Thomas Merton

Thomas Merton

Hermit at the Heart of Things

By J.S. Porter

NOVALIS

© 2008 Novalis, Saint Paul University, Ottawa, Canada

Cover design: Audrey Wells
Layout: Audrey Wells, Francine Petitclerc
Cover images: Kevin Burns
Interior images: Kevin Burns, except page 215: courtesy of New Directions
Publishing Corp.

Business Offices:
Novalis Publishing Inc.
10 Lower Spadina Avenue, Suite 400
Toronto, Ontario, Canada
M5V 2Z2

Novalis Publishing Inc.
4475 Frontenac Street
Montréal, Québec, Canada
H2H 2S2

Phone: 1-800-387-7164
Fax: 1-800-204-4140
E-mail: books@novalis.ca
www.novalis.ca

Library and Archives Canada Cataloguing in Publication

Porter, J. S.
    Thomas Merton : hermit at the heart of things / J.S. Porter.

ISBN 978-2-89646-008-3

    1. Merton, Thomas, 1915–1968. 2. Trappists–United States–Biography.
3. Spiritual life–Catholic Church. I. Title.

BX4705.M542P67 2008   271'.12502   C2008-900765-4

Printed in Canada.

We acknowledge the financial support of the Government of Canada through
the Book Publishing Industry Development Program (BPIDP) for our
publishing activities.

5   4   3   2   1   12   11   10   09   08

For Cheryl, who taught me
"the chomp chomp umm good *lip-puckered*
'Aaahhhh!' to life."

I have become an explorer for you, a searcher in realms which you are not able to visit ... I have been summoned to explore a desert area of man's heart in which explanations no longer suffice, and in which one learns that only experience counts.

Thomas Merton in an August 21, 1967 letter to Dom Francis Decroix in response to a request from Paul VI for a "message of contemplatives to the world."

Contents

Preface

Body to Body:
Thomas Merton & Henri Nouwen

For to write is to love: it is to inquire and to praise, to confess
and to appeal.—*Journals VI*

Two bestselling twentieth-century writers on spirituality—Thomas Merton and Henri Nouwen—ever fresh, ever beginning, chortle their way into our century. Catholic columnist and educator Father Ronald Rolheiser calls Nouwen the Kierkegaard of our time. In the intensity and ferocity of his self-interrogations and his radical call to live, not merely speak, the Gospel, he is. Merton, or Father Louis, as he was known by his fellow monks, is a little harder to classify. Monk, artist, poet, contemplative, social and literary critic, he strides through life and letters with the voraciousness of a William Blake. Baroness Catherine de Hueck Doherty, the founder of Friendship House in Harlem, calls him "The Man with Deep-Seeing Eyes."

Merton and Nouwen, sometimes gently, sometimes fiercely, grab the reader by the shoulders and shake. Wake up! they shout. They call on readers to live more fully, live more abundantly. They issue personal invitations to radical transformation. You don't so much read them to become more enlightened, although they both make contributions to your enlightenment. You read them to transform yourself. They are catalysts for transformation. Live zestfully, they say. Be awake and aware. "Come," they say, "here is the water of life. Dance in it."

A French-born poet-monk in the ascetic Cistercian Order who engages in politics and a Dutch psychologist-priest who leaves his teaching at Yale for life alongside people with disabilities are a fascinating pair. Merton with his emblems, seeds and raids. Nouwen with his clowns, icons and cups. Both men have what Merton, in a kind of

Beat lingo, calls "the chomp chomp *umm good* lip-puckered 'Aaahhhh!' to life."

Fittingly, many of Merton's posthumously published private journals have script superimposed on his face and body, as if in acknowledgment that words constitute his body as much as blood and bone. The body as a scriptorium. His word-inscribed face brings to mind a character in Joyce's *Finnegans Wake*, whose work is written "over every square inch of the only foolscap available, his own body." Thomas Merton and Henri Nouwen sketch dozens of self-portraits and make scores of body prints. Each time they pick up a pen or clack on the typewriter, they bring a new face into being. They manage to get their bodies on the page, their hearts and minds and spirits on the page. Through voice they achieve presence. That's why, when you meet Merton or Nouwen on the page, you feel as if you've met them in the flesh.

Merton and Nouwen remain spiritual presences in our world. In Nouwen's word, they remain *fruitful*. Merton is the silent monk who never shuts up, the solitary who clings to the world. He's the poet, in Father Daniel Berrigan's phrasing, who writes "an enormous unpruned lifelong diary of everything; trial and error and mood and conquest and pratfalls. And now and again, the midair triple somersault cannons into our hands." Nouwen is the solitary explorer, the shy talker, the vulnerable man of strength. Both take vows of conversation with the world. Nouwen, nearing the end of his life, takes a further vow to feed, bathe, dress and be completely responsible for one physically needy person by the name of Adam at L'Arche

Daybreak in Toronto. They follow the secret directive of the universe: grow or die.

For the most part, they write little books you can hold in your hand, although since his death Merton's publishers have sometimes inflated his little books into single-volume big books, as in the collected poetry, the collected literary essays, and the almost collected social and political essays. Both men are wounded in different ways, and both are tremendously productive. They question, doubt and struggle with such ferocity that neither will end up as a piece of plastic in a Catholic devotional shop. They're too wild and too unpredictable to be corralled in a box; too flawed and gloriously human.

Merton the scholar and Nouwen the academic find ways of speaking to large numbers of people without scholarly or academic language. They find a way to speak honestly and open-heartedly despite, or maybe because of, their ongoing crises and struggles to be fully human. They reach out across religious and secular divides.

Merton, in particular, begins an interfaith dialogue unequalled in his time or ours. He has an enormous gift for friendship. He makes friends with strangers, and then shares experiences of the sacred with them. Merton calls this practice of converting strangers into friends "the theology of encounter." You see this method of personal contact, relationship and friendship in his exchanges with Buddhists D.T. Suzuki in New York City, Thich Nhat Hanh at Gethsemani, and the Dalai Lama in Dharmsala, India. "One cannot understand Buddhism until one meets it in this existential manner, in a person in whom it is alive," he writes about Suzuki. Merton meets the living Buddha in the three wise men of the East, and they meet the living Christ in him.

I never met Thomas Merton, but I've walked where he walked on the Gethsemani grounds. I've seen the loblolly pines he planted around a cabin that turned out to be his hermitage. I've met him on the page where millions of others have met him. I've never formally studied him, never taught him, but I've read him with attention for a long time. I turn to him as one outsider to another.

Nouwen and Merton met, and Nouwen ended up writing a little book on him. What struck Nouwen about Merton was his ordinariness. He didn't stand out in any way. Nouwen wasn't even sure at first if the man he was talking to was Merton. "Merton looked like a farmer interrupting his work in the barn. He was dressed in blue jeans and a workman's shirt and talked in a very down-to-earth way about people and events that came up in conversation." Nouwen concludes, "Nothing pious, nothing 'spiritual,' nothing very 'uplifting'."

If I want to immerse myself in spiritual thought, I tend to soak in Nouwen or Merton. Both have the gift to incarnate speech, the ability to somehow underwrite their words with their flesh, with their own living experience. A recent compilation of Merton's writings conveniently divides his work between the autobiographical and the spiritual. But the two are always one. Merton's autobiographical writing is spiritual; his spiritual writings are autobiographical. The same may be said of Nouwen. Both live purpose-driven lives, and their purpose is to share their lives with the world.

Merton and Nouwen write from their bodies and their senses, from their whole being. For both, Christianity is less a body of beliefs than it is a body of actions and behaviours; it has to do with going the second mile, turning the other cheek, welcoming strangers, feeding the hungry, clothing the naked, visiting the sick and the imprisoned, forgiving seventy times seven. In the radical and revolutionary presence of Christ, the times are always changing. For both Merton and Nouwen, in their devotion to "the Christ of the burnt men," writing is action. They write to warn, to awaken, to encourage, to probe, to celebrate, to critique, to understand themselves and the world around them, and to love.

Merton's way of being in the world is to draw things into himself, to ingest them, to make them part of his body and personhood. His way of confronting problems or questions or tensions is to live them. If there is division in the Church, for example, he believes that he can in part overcome them personally by living the tensions. "If I can unite *in myself* the thought and the devotion of Eastern and Western Christendom, the Greek and the Latin Fathers, the Russians with the Spanish mystics, I can prepare in myself the reunion of divided Christians."

As Robert Inchausti writes in *Thomas Merton's American Prophecy*, in a radically plural and fragmented world, Merton "had begun the difficult task of uniting within himself all the various strands of a truly universal Catholicism ... through an existential appropriation of the experiential wisdom of many different people." His knowledge is relational, personal and experiential; it advances by encounter and relationship. What Merton knows, he knows by deep reading and reflection; he also knows by personal connection and friendship. His knowledge of Latin America deepens through his contact with Latin American poets. His knowledge of Judaism derives in part from his having close Jewish friends, including Robert Lax, who later converts to Catholicism. Significantly, when Merton is received into the Roman Catholic Church on November 16, 1938, in Provisional Baptism at Corpus Christi in New York City, his sponsor is Edward Rice and his three witnesses are three Jewish friends: Robert Lax, Robert Gerdy and Seymour Freedgood.

In affirming the other, Merton affirms himself: "If I affirm myself as a Catholic merely by denying all that is Muslim, Jewish, Protestant, Hindu, Buddhist, etc., in the end I will find that there is not much left for me to affirm as a Catholic: and certainly no breath of the Spirit with which to affirm it." Merton's way of being in the world seems hubristic and naive, but it is also powerful and effective. To a degree, in his own personhood, he unifies East and West by becoming a serious student of Zen Buddhism and its progenitor, Taoism. He crosses the Islamic-Christian divide in his fascinating correspondence with Abdul Aziz, a Sufi scholar living in Pakistan. He unifies the Church by respecting and writing about its many divergent traditions. When Merton says that he has the world in his bloodstream, he means it.

For Merton, as with Nouwen, writing is a way of loving, of expressing love. In words equally appropriate for Nouwen, Merton says in a phrase at once simple and profound, "... to write is to love." Merton writes effusively about what he loves and the people he loves, and with rage when the things he loves—the natural environment, the public good, the individual's soul—are put in danger. He deepens his understanding of the world by writing about it. He knows that he writes best when he writes about the things he loves: "ideas, places, certain persons—all very definite, individual, identifiable objects of love."

Writing, to Merton and Nouwen, is what a cane is to the blind; it's their way of tapping into the world and probing its mysteries while becoming more aware of its goodness. Patrick Hart and Jonathan Montaldo, editors of *The Intimate Merton*, the one-volume compilation of the complete personal journals, remark on how Merton falls into solitude and silence by writing about them. Their memorable phrase is "He wrote about silence to become silent." Writing brings him near the One he seeks, and puts him in a receptive state to receive creation's grace and bounty:

> [W]riting is one thing that gives me access to some real silence and solitude. Also I find that it helps me to pray, because when I pause at my work I find that the mirror inside me is surprisingly clean and deep and serene and God shines there and is immediately found, without hunting, as if He had come close to me while I was writing and I had not observed His coming …

What Merton seeks, and Nouwen, too, is "to put [himself] down on paper … with the most complete simplicity and integrity, masking nothing … without exaggeration, repetition, useless emphasis." Merton desires "a complete and holy transparency: living, praying, and writing in the light of the Holy Spirit … to become as plain as a Host in the hands of everybody." By the end of his short and interrupted life, he enfleshes a kind of holy transparency.

I

Always a Beginner

One cannot begin to face the real difficulties of the life of prayer and meditation unless one is first perfectly content to be a beginner ... [L]et us be convinced of the fact that we will never be anything else but beginners, all our life.
—*The Climate of Monastic Prayer*

"He's a Zorba monk."—Dan Pilling in conversation with the author

Thomas Merton: Open. Spontaneous. Honest. Disciplined. Self-critical. Searching. Smiles warmly. Laughs easily. These are a few of the modifiers I apply to him in conversation with my eighty-five-year-old mother from the north Irish fishing village of Portavogie. She has begun to read him for the first time. Other adjectives hover nearby: quick, enthusiastic, playful, idealizing, impulsive, stubborn and sometimes sharp-tongued, constantly growing. And then, I plunge into his heart: Word-centred. Book-built. Spirit-haunted. Sometimes I can convince myself that my life word—spiritbookword— is also his.

I say some more things to my diminutive, blue-eyed, white-haired mother with her beautiful sea-worn face. How in poetry Merton moves from the "poetry of the choir" to the "poetry of the desert" to the poetry of engagement and critique. How in prose he moves from self-satisfied piety to books of questions and struggles and redefinitions. His visual art evolves from risqué doodles to cartoons to figures of piety to "ciphers of energy." In his monastic life, he turns from an exclusive Roman Catholicism to an inclusive Christian humanism.

I can't think of another writer who grows so much and so deeply in so short a time. Think of the twenty years between the publication of *The Seven Storey Mountain* in 1948 to the journal entries in 1968 that form the basis of *The Asian Journal*, published after his death. Even in an eight-year period—from 1960 to 1968, the period I'll concentrate on in this book—the changes and growth are astounding. Many writers, in contrast, find what they can do early on, and keep doing it. They essentially write one book all their lives.

I put Mom onto Jim Forest's pictorial biography. The book has an intimacy about it, a friend writing about a friend. Forest may lack the detail and comprehensiveness of the Michael Mott biography, one of the great biographies of our time, but he successfully refashions Merton in image as much as word. The biography enables my mother to see Merton as well as hear him.

Forest's encounter with Merton is noteworthy. He enters a room filled with monks not knowing which one is Merton. One particular monk lies in kinks on the floor. That particular monk is Thomas Merton. Forest has his first meeting with a prostrate man laughing uproariously about himself and the world. Years after his encounter with Merton, the Dalai Lama remembers: "We were very serious in our discussions, but our nature, laughing, joking, teasing quickly came through …." This laughing man is also made real by Merton's letter to Baroness Catherine de Hueck Doherty on September 18, 1958:

> It certainly is a wonderful thing to wake up suddenly in the solitude of the woods and look up at the sky and see the utter nonsense of everything, including all the solemn stuff given out by professional asses about the spiritual life and simply to burst out laughing, and laugh and laugh with the sky and the trees because God is not in words, and not in systems, and not in liturgical movement, and not in "contemplation" with a big C, or in asceticism … not even in the apostolate …

Perhaps this is the laugh that Jim Forest, an Orthodox convert and fellow worker in the peace movement, heard on his first encounter with Merton.

Mom responds to Forest's book enthusiastically but also questioningly. "Isn't it a wasted life to shut yourself off in a monastery?" My mother, a tough-minded Protestant, asks the sort of questions the feisty Catholic theologian Rosemary Ruether once asked Merton in her correspondence with him. I explain that Merton writes to the world at large from his monastery, numerous friends come to visit, and he has contact and intercourse with his fellow monks. "How's that so different from us?" I ask my mother. "We love a few within our circle; we have impact on a few within that circle." Merton's circle is broader than most and it goes on rippling across time and geography to new generations.

When I pick up an essay by bell hooks, an African-American feminist lesbian, I find these words: "All around me I feel surrounded by the spirits of writers and thinkers from the past (some living, most dead) whose work still lives for me: Thomas Merton, Eudora Welty, Norman Mailer, Jack Kerouac." Merton's work still lives for me. I'm drawn to his politics, prayers, confessions, meditations and art.

Merton is a Zorbamonk, a dancer who reads, a dancer who studies, a dancer who prays. He continues to pop up in unexpected places. Open Oprah's magazine and there he is. You see him quoted in *Adbusters* or maybe *Harper's*. You read him in a book on Yoga. He gets around.

After Forest, Mom picks up *The Seven Storey Mountain*, the book Brother Christopher describes as "the story of how a young bohemian intellectual full of passion and fire gradually found his way to becoming a monk." She finds it a more challenging read than the biography, but equally worthwhile. "I think the monastery was too hard on him," she says. "They took advantage of him."

I respond, "Keep in mind, Mom, that Merton wouldn't have been an easy person to live with. He lived with conflicting impulses and tensions. The monastery gave him structure and stability." What I don't tell her is that the more one reads Merton, the more one develops a certain sympathy for his superior, Dom James. I sense that my responses to my mother's questions are inadequate. But what matters is that she, like so many before her, has been bitten. She has brought Merton into her life; he's now someone about whom she cares enough to have an opinion.

"*The Seven Storey Mountain* is a very sad book," she tells me. "All that loss." I think back to my own first reaction. When I first read *The Seven Storey Mountain*, Thomas Merton's official autobiography, the narrative didn't strike me as unusually sad, even when it dwelt on loss and disruption. Then I listened to a professional reader read me the narrative aloud and it seemed very sad. When the story entered my ear directly, without the intervention of the eye, the story at times seemed painfully sad, even unbearably sad.

There's a way in which *The Seven Storey Mountain* is one of the saddest stories ever told. It is a story about loss. The loss of a mother. The loss of a father. The loss of grandparents. The loss of a brother. The sadness builds in the narrative until you're not sure as a reader if you can take one more death, one more loss. In the original narrative, Merton's *Mountain* ends at the death of his brother and his grieving for his deceased brother. Merton is a man who learns to live with lifelong scars.

Merton's way of handling the sadness—his conversion to Catholicism and his entering the Cistercian Order where, in theory, one no longer needs to speak—seems on one level to be the equivalent of his brother, John Paul, enlisting in the Canadian Air Force: an act of desperation. The self has been badly damaged and bruised, so the thing to do is to put the cloak of structure around it. The wounds are bleeding, so wrap the bandage of the strict Cistercians around it. A young man who has had his family tree cut down before his eyes needs whatever shelter he can find.

Merton in *The Seven Storey Mountain* seeks certitudes, things that won't change or disappear. He accordingly defines himself by what he isn't. He isn't a Protestant or a Buddhist or a political thinker or even a poet. He is a Catholic monk in the Cistercian order. By the time of *The Asian Journal*, twenty years later, Merton defines himself by the breadth of his embrace, and he embraces almost everything he rejected earlier. He builds a self on the principle of inclusion rather than exclusion.

I situate Merton for Mom in time and space. At the height of Merton's literary production in the 1960s, Bob Dylan is singing "The Times They Are a-Changing," the Beatles have written "Hey Jude," the Vietnam War rages, Adolf Eichmann goes on trial, the Bay of Pigs invasion seizes newspaper headlines, the Cuban missile crisis terrifies a continent, the Soviets launch the first man into space, the Black Panther Party is formed, Dr. Martin Luther King

Jr. hits the streets, there are riots in Chicago, Jack Kennedy takes a bullet in Dallas and his younger brother takes one in Los Angeles. A large portion of what I remind her of, Merton himself references in *The Asian Journal.*

I tell her that Gethsemani, where Merton spends most of his adult life, is a few miles south of Bardstown, one of Kentucky's oldest towns and the site of the largest bourbon distillery in the world. The monastery is about fifty miles south of Louisville, the state capital. The monastery is located in what are called the Kentucky knobs: gentle hills, farm lands and a primarily deciduous forest. Merton's hermitage, an easy walking distance from the monastery, is surrounded by broad-leafed trees like beech and oak canopying snakes and rodents, and the pine trees he helped plant. Notwithstanding periodic visits to a Louisville hospital, a few days in New York City and locations visited as part of his journey to Thailand, Merton hardly ever leaves his monastic home.

Mom asks how he was able to write so much, and accomplish so much. Her question is one that legions of Merton readers pose. I don't know the answer. I make some guesses. He doesn't have a spouse or the responsibilities of children. He doesn't have a nine-to-five job. He doesn't watch television; he doesn't go to movies; he doesn't play video games. Distractions and diversions don't blacken his day. He has space to study and to grow. He gets by on very little sleep. He also reads with his teeth. He bangs on the typewriter with his fingers on fire.

I say these things to my mother, and sense that Merton now matters to her because she knows that he matters to her son. She encounters him partly through Forest's words and images, and partly through the inadequacies of my voice and memory. Something of his spirit comes through to her in my flawed conversation about him.

People find their way to Merton in different ways. My friend Mark Garber found him in the Korean War. He carried *The Seven Storey Mountain* in his knapsack. Black Power leader Eldridge Cleaver found him in prison, in the same book. I too find him in a book.

In 1978, my friend David Charles Wagg gives me a paperback copy of Edward Rice's *The Man in the Sycamore Tree: The Good Times and Hard Life of Thomas Merton*. "The Man in the Sycamore Tree" is a title Merton gives to one of his early unpublished novels. The book has a $1.95 sticker on it. Beneath the sticker is the price of the hardback original: $7.95. I don't remember hearing anything or reading anything about Merton prior to the Rice biography.

Thirty years later, I'm still hanging out with this monk, this poet, this Zorba, who metaphorically dances on the beach like Anthony Quinn in the movie and studies in the kitchen like the young intellectual called Boss. I'm beginning again. For a time, I think I should call this book *Thomas Merton: Zorba Monk*. Or, to steal a different phrase from Robert Lax than the one I've chosen, call it *Thomas Merton, Superabundantly Alive*.

Edward Rice visualizes Merton as a cross between a San Franciscan longshoreman (an Eric Hoffer) and a farmer from Nelson County (one of Merton's self-charac-terizations). Facially he looks a little like Picasso or Henry Miller. In stranger ways than I'm able to articulate, this monk in the Order of Cistercians of the Strict Observance has become a kind of parallel life for me.

Rice's biography, the first full biography of the poet-monk, was written in 1970. It has a sixties stylistic energy and a sixties cluster of concerns: war, peace, spirituality and activism. An unspoken question runs through the book: How does one maintain peace and faith in a world governed by profit and greed?

"What has no price has no value ... what cannot be sold is not real, so that the only way to make something *actual* is to place it on the market," Merton declaims in "Rain and the Rhinoceros." We live in a time when even water is put into plastic bottles and sold to the public. What ought to be the property of all is packaged by some and sold to all. What once was a festival, according to Merton's sacramental vision, is now a commodity. Merton must have had a premonition of the commodification of water. His opening line in "Rain and the Rhinoceros" reads, "Let me say this before rain becomes a utility that they can plan and distribute for money."

Rice's title suggests a little man who climbs high in order to see the coming of the Christ. The title also points to a man who wants to see things; he just needs to be in the right perch. Much of Merton's life is concerned with seeing things clearly: power structures, destructive impediments to societal and individual growth, the importance of ceremony and ritual, the need for silence and solitude. He finds the right perch from which to see himself and the world. He is under constant self-revision. In the twenty-seven years before he enters the Abbey of Our Lady of Gethsemani and in his twenty-seven years after, Merton experiences a mixture of good and hard times. He also discovers home, a place where he can experience "all the times and moods of one good place."

I can't remember if the biography David gave me was new or used. He frequently passes along books, both new and used, to me. As a Christmas present ten years after the gift of Rice, in order to keep my feet planted on Merton's ground, he gives me a composite Merton biography, *Merton by Those Who Knew Him Best*, edited by Paul Wilkes and including tributes by the folksinger Joan Baez and the poet and publisher Lawrence Ferlinghetti. David has a knack for knowing my tendency to enter a writer's body of work by way of biography first.

Unlike a Faulkner, say—a novelist about whom Merton wrote perspicaciously—whose characters stand independently of his person, Merton's body of work is best read within the flow of his life. You need to know what is going on in his life to appreciate more fully, at any given moment, what is going on in his work. Merton changes from year to year, month to month, even day to day, at times. He has a "need for constant self-revision and growth." His ideas "are always changing." He may be accused of inconsistency, but he "will no longer be there to hear the accusation." He'll have moved on.

You need to read Merton twice: once by biography and chronology in a temporal-spatial continuum and once by the particular mood-driven, time-sculpted work you have in your hand. The work and the life meld like chiaroscuro. For every utterance, you need to read him with three questions constantly in mind: What's the date and context? What's the mood? Who's the audience?

Edward Rice, along with Robert Lax, is one of Merton's classmates at Columbia University; they work together on the college magazine *Jester*, for which Lax is the editor and Merton the art editor, and they remain close friends throughout Merton's short life. Rice later becomes the editor of *Jester*. He also publishes a number of Merton's important social and political statements, including "Religion and the Bomb," in a new ecumenical magazine he founds called *Jubilee*. Rice conceives *Jubilee* as "a Catholic magazine with a pictorial format and a commitment to the Church's social teachings." From 1953 to 1967, Rice edits the magazine and receives over two dozen submissions from Merton.

In *The Man in the Sycamore Tree*, Rice is particularly good at responding to Merton's visual work. He notes, for example, that Merton, after his schoolboy days, takes up drawing again in the fifties, working in "an oriental, calligraphic style which was part derivation from Chinese ideograms, part symbols of buildings and landscapes."

The artwork, particularly his late drawings and photographs, still stands as a good introduction to Merton. The wordless Merton, the image-making Merton, is as important as the worded Merton. His Zen ink marks and his Shaker photographs are "collaborations with solitude" and "footprints of the unconscious." One sees the connections of things, drawings with photography, artwork with final poems, art with his spirituality. All are articulations of the mystery they derive from and dissolve into.

Look at the photographs: *Cloister Niche* with its apparition like a third person, *White Chair*, *Stone Wall*, *Cleft Rock*, *Birds*, *Mt. Kanchenjunga*, *Tibetan Child*, all Shaker-simple, all in *The Geography of Holiness*. Merton frames simple images. He writes simple words.

I look again at Rice's selection of Merton's calligraphic reproductions and student drawings along with striking photographs of Merton himself: Merton standing on the porch of his hermitage, Merton stoking the fire, Merton reading, Merton in his toque and jean jacket looking out the window smiling, Merton walking in the woods by the pond, Merton clowning under a statue of Saint Benedict. Rice's style is light and journalistic. He appropriately calls his book "An Entertainment, with Photographs." The book touches upon Merton's Columbia University years, his monastic years, his civil rights engagement, his preparation for Asia and encounters with the Dalai Lama.

Rice emphasizes the Zen Merton, the mischievous Merton, the politically conscious Merton. He is surprisingly weak on the Christian Merton. One of Rice's sectional headings reads "The Making of a Beatnik, Peacenik Trappist Buddhist Monk." The Merton that Rice presents is both seer and activist, monk and poet.

You can picture Rice's Merton speaking out to CNN or in *The New York Times* on post-Katrina America: "People demand that the government 'interfere' in nothing, just pour money into the armament industry and provide a strong police for 'security'. But stay out of everything else! No interference in medicine, mental health, education … Never was a country at once shrewder and less wise—shrewd in nonessentials and lunatic in essentials." Put that in neon: Never was a country at once shrewder and less wise.

Rice is also effective in presenting Merton's understanding of Western and North American "mythdreams" in which we delude ourselves into thinking that others operate out of mythologies while we "are utterly scientific" and "have no myths," which in itself is one of our principal myths. He quotes Merton as saying that the reason communication is difficult across cultures is that we lack · "an ability to communicate also with something deeper in ourselves ... We are out of contact with our own depths. It is our primitive self which has become alien, hostile and strange."

Rice's tapas were enough for me at the time. I'd go on to fuller banquets later, but Rice's little book fed me sufficiently then. Eventually I moved on to the English journalist Monica Furlong's biography of Merton, the Canadian George Woodcock's biographical study of Merton as monk and poet, and then to Merton's *The Asian Journal*. Even so, for a long time, the Buddhist Merton was my Merton, the Rice Merton was my Merton. After *The Asian Journal*, I read Merton more or less chronologically backwards to *The Seven Storey Mountain*, his starting point and my end point. I read everything, as I'm inclined to do when I fall in love with a particular writer.

When I move from the photographs of Merton's sunny face to his revelatory words, the words that draw me in have to do with the honest acknowledgment of his shortcomings, even his own moral and physical wreckage—wreckage we all carry in our all-too-human wakes. Who would not be struck by the honesty of a man recording his fall from physical grace into the humiliations of middle age? "An arthritic hip; a case of chronic dermatitis ...;

sinusitis ...; lungs always showing up some funny shadow ...; perpetual diarrhea and a bleeding anus; most of my teeth gone; most of my hair gone; a chewed-up vertebra in my neck ... What an existence!" I identified then, and identify now, with his aches and his honest disclosure of them. Many of us, in Leonard Cohen's line, ache in the places where we used to play.

Merton owns a few paintings, an icon, a rosary. When he dies in Bangkok, the police estimate his net worth at ten dollars. Hardly a success in the world's eyes. In fact, throughout his life he regards the word *success* with contempt: "Be anything you like, be madmen, drunks, and bastards of every shape and form, but at all costs avoid one thing: success." Now, that's a statement for students to hear in their commencement addresses! Put that in neon, too. And connect it to Baudelaire's prose poem on the need for an ongoing drunkenness, the need for ecstasy, the need to be a Zorba, and you have a summons to students to begin again.

In giving an account to the American poet Louis Zukofsky of his starting and editing the literary journal *Monks Pond* in the last year of his life, Merton whimsically explains what matters in his editing life: "No money involved anywhere." Instead: "Poems, creative things, Asian texts, blues, koans, ghost dances, all to be crammed into four issues." Again, the word *dance* crystallizes in Merton's thought and sentences. Think of seed 39, The General Dance, which concludes *New Seeds of Contemplation* and invites all to join the cosmic dance: "For the world and time are the dance of the Lord in emptiness."

Merton says yes and no to the world. He says "NO to the concentration camps, the aerial bombardments, the staged political trials, the judicial murders, the racial injustices, the economic tyrannies ... the whole socio-economic apparatus which seems geared for nothing but global destruction in spite of all its fair words in favor of peace." "I make," he continues in introductory remarks to the Japanese edition of *The Seven Storey Mountain*, "monastic silence a protest against the lies of politicians, propagandists, and agitators." He notes in the same preface that the faith in which he believes "is also invoked by many who believe in war, believe in racial injustices, believe in self-righteous and lying forms of tyranny." Merton says that his life must then "be a protest against these also."

Merton isn't afraid to say no, but neither is he hesitant in saying yes. He says "YES to all that is good in the world and in man ... YES to all that is beautiful in nature ...." One of the beautiful things of his journals is that, whatever is going on in his life, he's never too busy to observe what's happening to a bird or butterfly. The weather also figures prominently in his writing. Turn to the recent compilation *When the Trees Say Nothing* for a reminder of Merton's ecstatic celebration of the natural world. " ... YES to all the men and women who are my brothers and sisters in the world ...." You don't have to read much Merton before being swept up in his great zest for life and living things, his great dance upon the earth.

I offer this personal note because so often readers of Merton share stories of how (when and where) they first met the round-faced monk. I think that the verb *to meet* is the right one; you don't read Merton, you meet him. When readers go to Merton conferences, they tell each other stories of their first encounters, a kind of ongoing testimonial to a poet-monk who continues to influence human lives. I've spoken to Merton readers who met Merton through their work in trade unions, civil rights and the peace movement. I've listened to business leaders, environmentalists and homemakers tell me how Merton turned them around in some fundamental way.

What continues to astonish me about Merton is how he continues to change human lives: how people get politically involved because of him, how people return to faith because of him, how people continue to draw sustenance from his life as if he were still alive in the world, still doing work in the world. When I read Hemingway, as much as I admire his style and literature, I don't feel that I'm reading a living person. With Merton, I'm not so sure. My eighty-five-year-old mother says one of the reasons Merton still has presence in the world is that his world remains our world. Events such as the Vietnam War, civil rights battles and the supremacy of technology are still in public memory. War, state-generated fear and government propaganda remain a significant part of our lives.

Maybe part of the Merton magic has to do with his always being a beginner, someone who comes at life as if he were a stranger to it and is beginning to find his way in it for the first time. He takes dramatic turns in his life. He starts over. He begins again.

This idea of being a beginner is both profoundly Buddhist and Christian. I recall Merton's words in *The Climate of Monastic Prayer*: "One cannot begin to face the real difficulties of the life of prayer and meditation unless one is first perfectly content to be a beginner ... let us be convinced of the fact that we will never be anything else but beginners, all our life." His words echo Rainer Maria Rilke, a poet he lectures on in his talks to novices: "If the Angel deigns to come it will because you have convinced her, not by tears but by your humble resolve to be always beginning; to be a beginner."

Somehow, David putting Rice's book in my hands many years ago gives me a sense that Merton is always beginning, always coming at experience in fresh ways, experimenting, trying things out. Ten years after receiving David's gift, I write *The Thomas Merton Poems* in 1988 in an attempt to reproject Merton's voice and preoccupations.

Now, thirty years after my first encounter with Merton through Rice's entertainment, I construct a word-collage of Merton's many-sided fullness. Merton the contemplative and activist. Merton the poet, reader and translator. Merton the letter writer and tone meister. Merton the intellectual and lover. Merton the synthesizer and journal keeper. These are the main stitches of my book. The counter-stitches are Merton the visual artist, the dancer and the beginner. Others knit different fabrics. Merton the monk, Merton the mystic, Merton the Christian humanist, and so on. You knit what you can according to your own comfort and experience, your own shortcomings and limitations.

I emphasize the sixties Merton, whereas others may emphasize the pre-sixties Merton. The sixties, it seems to me, are when he is at the heart of most things. I make his last book, *The Asian Journal*, a central concern whereas others make his first autobiography, *The Seven Storey Mountain*, more central. My account of Merton—snapshots in nine poses—gradually slouches eastward, as his life did in that last great open-hearted embrace of life. Even though my hermit ends in Asia, as the real hermit did, it's not so much the Asian Merton I lift up for your consideration, or the European Merton; rather, it's the American Merton, Merton of the Americas, that I underscore.

Merton is a daunting mountain. You make your own individual pathway across his life. You climb a slope, a peak perhaps, but the bulk of him remains unclimbed. What Whitman said about himself, you can as truthfully say about Merton: he is vast, he contains multitudes. I leave vast tracts of his life and work untouched by comment. I leave realms of his personhood unexplored. On confident days, I think that I've drawn a portrait of a monk. On insecure days, I think that I've drawn nobody's face but my own—my longing, my emotional needs, my desperate lunge for home.

For those of you reading about Merton for the first time, my hope is that you continue on the Merton path to wherever it leads you. For those of you familiar with Merton, my hope is that you begin again.

II

Contemplative & Activist

The monastic life is in a certain sense scandalous. The monk is precisely a man *who has no specific task*. He is liberated from the routines and servitudes of organized human activity in order to *be free*. Free for what? Free to see, free to praise, free to understand, free to love.

—*Contemplation in a World of Action*

Thomas Merton is a poet-monk, an artist-monk. Secular France gives greater weight to one side of the hyphen than the other. A plaque on his family home in Prades reads "Ici est né Thomas Merton, Écrivain Américain." The French town of St. Antonin, where Merton attended a nearby school, has a plaque that reads "Thomas Merton, Écrivain." Religious America tends to shift the emphasis to the monk side of the hyphen. Clearly he is both writer and monk. He is also a contemplative-activist. You need to do justice to both sides of Merton's hyphens.

In his early years, and specifically on November 27, 1941, Merton, in *The Secular Journal*, weighs the merits of joining Friendship House in Harlem, under the leadership of Catherine de Hueck Doherty, against the Trappist monastery of Gethsemani near Bardstown, Kentucky. "Today I think: should I be going to Harlem, or to the Trappists?" He sees his choice starkly. Either he becomes a Catholic activist and works with the poor, or he becomes a contemplative and lives with his monastic brothers.

He chooses "the center of America." In part, I suspect, because he believes that it will hold him together just as it holds the country together: "I had wondered what was holding the country together, what has been keeping the universe from cracking in pieces and falling apart. It is places like this monastery ...." He needs to mend his fractures.

As the years advance, starkness gives way to something more mottled. Merton sees ways of integrating prayer with politics, of being simultaneously a contemplative and an activist. He resolves the tension between contemplation and action in much the same way he resolves the tension between poetry and monkhood. He embraces both. He wisely sees that his natural way of being monastic grafts more than it excises: "Some conclusions: Literature, contemplative solitude, Latin America, Asia, Zen, Islam etc., all these things come together in my life. It would be madness for me to attempt to create a monastic life for myself by excluding all these."

To his list of passions and commitments, he adds political activism, and aligns himself with Dorothy Day of the Catholic Worker movement and the Berrigan brothers, for whom the New Testament is much more concerned with social justice than it is with homosexuality and abortion. Merton's way of being active in the world is to write about it.

As a Zorbamonk, Merton marries dance with study, carnival with contemplation and critique. His friend and teacher Mark Van Doren describes Merton as having "a merry mind with knives in it." His friend Robert Lax speaks of his superabundance. The art critic Roger Lipsey writes of his "surplus," "a surplus of energy and intelligence, inquiry and camaraderie."

Merton's activism arises from his contemplative calling. His authenticity stems from his commitment to monastic life. In a conversation quoted by his friend Amiya Chakravarty, Merton says, "As a Trappist monk, my life too is one piece … If I make cheese it has to be right, if I work on the land I draw a straight furrow, if I sing the Gregorian chant it has to be authentic." He authenticates his words by living them. He is a twentieth-century American poet living by the traditions of twelfth-century monastic principles.

According to Brother Patrick Hart, Merton's fellow monk at Gethsemani and his private secretary for the final years of his life, Merton exhorts his monastic brothers to return to Benedictine spirituality "as this was spelled out so well by our Cistercian fathers in the twelfth century."

> Before Merton's time, at Gethsemani at least and probably in lots of other Trappist monasteries, we were still living the seventeenth-century Trappist reform. Merton felt that there was more to monasticism than that. He wanted to get back to the pure sources … he wanted to get beyond all the rigidity, and to do this he even went back beyond the Cistercians to the roots of the Christian monastic movement, to John Cassian and the Desert Fathers ….

The Cistercian day consists of manual labour, personal reflection, and private and public prayer. Merton's working day as a contemplative differs from mine and probably yours, not only in the time he gets up and the time he goes to bed, but also in what he does in his waking hours. He records his hours as a hermit in a letter to his Sufi correspondent, Abdul Aziz.

He goes to bed about 7:30 at night and rises about 2:30 in the morning. On rising he says part of the canonical Office, consisting of psalms, lessons, etc. Then he takes an hour and a quarter for meditation. He follows the meditations with some Bible reading and then has breakfast if it is not a busy day. Breakfast consists of bread and tea or coffee, with perhaps a piece of fruit or some honey. With breakfast he begins reading and continues reading and studying until sunrise.

At sunrise he says another Office of psalms, etc., then begins his manual work, which includes sweeping, cleaning, cutting wood. If he has time, he writes a few letters, usually short. After this, he goes down to the monastery to say Mass. After Mass he takes one cooked meal in the monastery. Then he returns immediately to the hermitage, usually without seeing or speaking to anyone. On returning to the hermitage, he does some light reading, and then says another Office about one o'clock. This is followed by another hour or more of meditation.

He then works at his writing, an hour and a half or two hours at most each day. Following that, it being now late afternoon (about four), he says another Office of psalms, and prepares a light supper. He cooks minimally, usually only tea or soup, and makes a sandwich of some sort. Thus he has only a minimum of dishes to wash. After supper, he has another hour or more of meditation before going to bed.

As an ordinary monk, his day would have varied slightly from this pattern. Less time to himself, more time in the choir loft, more time in the vegetable fields and, while he was master of novices and later master of scholastics, more time preparing lectures and interacting with fellow monks. In either case, monk or hermit, he fills the day with prayer or meditation and the singing or reading of psalms.

If Merton doesn't live a life of silence, solitude and study, if he doesn't struggle with his vows of poverty, chastity, obedience, stability and conversion of manners, if he doesn't work hard physically in the fields and subject himself to a simple life of prayer, he is simply one more poet, one more commentator on the world scene. His uniqueness is to speak to the world from within the confines of what my daughter calls his prison cell.

The more Merton withdraws from the world—first into the monastery and the priesthood, and then to his cabin hermitage—the more he engages with the world. Through his own wounds, he speaks to the wounds of the world; and through his abandonment of the world, he draws closer to the beauty and goodness of the world. In being both a contemplative and an activist, he gradually evolves into Robert Lax's "hermit at the heart of things."

To encompass the wholeness of Merton, you'd need more than one hyphen. He is a calligrapher and a photographer. He is a journal keeper, a poet, a letter writer, an essayist, a failed novelist, a once-only dramatist, a social and literary critic, a translator and a theological interpreter, a political commentator. He is a man for whom the French phrase *touche-à-tout* seems specifically designed. He touches everything.

Primarily, however, he is a monk. As Jim Forest reminds us, "He spent far more time at Mass, in prayer, and in meditation than in writing books and letters or doing anything else likely to bring him to public attention." At times, Merton may seem like a real life Pi, the main character in Yann Martel's *Life of Pi* who considers himself to be a Hindu, a Muslim and a Christian. But he always remains a Roman Catholic priest in the Cistercian Order. His deep-rootedness in his own tradition allows him to branch out to others in other faiths. His commitment to his monastery is his still point in the turning world.

To grasp Merton's many-sidedness, think of a David Hockney photo collage where many images flow into one.

Think of Eugene Ralph Meatyard's deliberately out-of-focus photographs of Merton playing the bongo drums: a man in action, a man in a blur of activities, and yet a man given completely to the stillness of reading and writing. Merton, as much a reader-monk as he is a writer-monk, is a fluid monk, a changing monk, a constantly growing and revising monk. When you read him, you need to have the date of his words in front of you. But you also need to go back to his ground, to what grounded him, his monastic life of prayer, service and study.

According to his friend Dorothy Day, "He had known much pain, and he knew how to lift pain from others." His teacher and friend Mark Van Doren, who wrote three poems to Merton—"Once in Kentucky," "Death of a Monk (T.M.)" and "Prophet"—powerfully intones, "He gave us again the quietness of our minds." Van Doren knew that the quiet had been earned: "But of course it was terrible to be where he had been:/To have dug those utterly simple sentences out of the/soul's grave." Merton learns to write powerful messages in simple sentences.

He also learns to concentrate less on himself and more on the world. He abandons the role of bystander and adopts the role of participant. He draws knives from his merry mind. Through letters and tracts—given monastic restrictions, Merton's only permissable form of action—he adds his voice to the peace movement and the civil rights movement.

His August 23, 1961, letter to Dorothy Day announces a new direction:

> As for writing: I don't feel that I can in conscience, at a time like this, go on writing just about things like meditation …

I cannot bury my head in a lot of rather tiny and second-ary monastic studies either. I think I have to face the big issues, the life-and-death issues: and this is what everyone is afraid of.

Merton doesn't let go of his meditation—or, for that matter, his monastic studies—but he does hurl himself into the battles of his time with increased ferocity.

If you want comfort, you won't turn to Merton. He's more likely to give you disquiet. The world is complicated and messy and difficult. What works once in one situation may not work in another. What helps sometimes may hinder at other times. Things are naturally in flow. They harden, if they harden at all, because we force them to.

If you want certainty, you won't turn to Thomas Merton. He doesn't give you that. In fact, he may give you its opposite: doubt. Listen again to his last recorded prayer: "Let us therefore join hands ... I will try to say something that comes out of the depths of our hearts. I ask you to concentrate on the love that is in you, that is in us all. I have no idea what I am going to say. I am going to be silent a minute, and then I will say something." He doesn't tell you to believe or what to believe unless you're looking at his very early work; he's more likely to encourage skepticism and radical questioning than mindless obedience.

If you come to Merton, you come for the tensions, the ironies, the ambivalences, the paradoxes. You come into a struggling human being's life and work; you enter into his clear and troubled mind, his scarred and festive body. You enter into his talkative silence, his crowded solitude, his fleshy spirituality. You embrace his oxymorons, his humble egoism, his garrulous silence, his gregarious solitariness.

He's a shy exhibitionist and a conservative revolutionary. He invites you into his life by a kind of incarnational magic. I am you, he says time and again, and you are me. What moves in you moves in me.

Merton's mission as explorer and searcher of the desert regions of the heart is to undergo change and transformation and to write about the changes and transformations in such a way that you wonder if you're part of the transformation, too. The Merton magic is that in transforming himself and writing about the transformation as it occurs, he transforms you as well as himself.

I come to his many-sided life with my hands open. He has much to give. The letter writer writes to children as well as to the famous around the world. The journal keeper gives a full record of what it's like to be alive and engaged in our distempered time. The metaphor maker draws the world. The tone meister finds a way of speaking to the world in a kind of pillow talk, an intimate whispering. He speaks in a small, personal voice. The intellectual tackles the issues of his and our day. The poet and the reader-translator of poetry makes foreign things familiar.

Each part connects to the whole in Merton. Everything, as Robert Lax observed, is connected: the calligraphies, the photographs, the poems, the politics, the meditations, the prayers, the journals. They're all parts of an integrated whole. You need to read him holistically.

Brother Patrick Hart slightly remakes Lax's valuable insight in his interview with Sr. Mary Margaret Funk in the context of a discussion on Celtic monasticism:

But there was his interest in the early Celtic monasticism of the sixth century. He was digging into that, teaching himself Early Irish so he could translate their poetry. He had an inquisitive mind that just knew no bounds. He was a kind of universal person.

There's no one quite like him. Never in my life have I met anyone with such a variety of interests, so many. And he could see connections among them all. That was the thing —he was always bringing out the connections.

I turn to his prayers and poems, his journals, letters and literary criticism for succour and sustenance. My Merton consists of a small body of work, a small collection of words, more Klee than Rothko. I don't need the sixty or so volumes by his hand and the hundred or so about him by other hands. One can only keep so much.

These are some of the works I return to: "Hagia Sophia" from *Emblems of a Season of Fury*. Did he ever write more beautiful and more deeply contemplative prose than "Hagia Sophia"? Did he ever conceive of a more powerful book title than "Emblems of a Season of Fury"? It's important, by the way, to read Merton as far as possible in the way he arranged himself to be read. In *Emblems*, the meditations belong with the furies, his harmonious Sophia with his discordant chants. This slim volume also houses his analysis of the world situation of his time in the form of "A Letter to Pablo Antonio Cuadra Concerning Giants" alongside his poems, and translations of primarily Latin American poets, including Cuadra himself. If you read only the anthologized works of Merton disconnected from their original presentation, you miss out on how one piece of his literature speaks to another.

Day of a Stranger, a brief journal of a single day in his life, the whole mishmash of his passions and interests in a few pages. The calligraphies in *Raids on the Unspeakable* and *A Catch of Anti-Letters* (the Merton-Lax correspondence of 1962–1967). "Notes for a Philosophy of Solitude" in *Disputed Questions*. "Rain and the Rhinocheros," an essay from *Raids*. *Conjectures of a Guilty Bystander*, the book Brother Patrick Hart recommends for newcomers to Merton.

Emblems of a Season of Fury in its entirety (a book of poems, translations, and prose pieces), which contains, to my mind, his best poetry—"Song for Nobody," "Song: If You Seek…," "Night-flowering Cactus," "Love Winter When the Plant Says Nothing," and "The Fall." His "Signatures: Notes on the Author's Drawings" in *Raids*. Passages from *The Asian Journal* (a Book of Everything). Passages from the personal journals, particularly *Turning Toward the World*, *Dancing in the Water of Life*, and *Learning to Love*, including his diary to M. Sections from *The Seven Storey Mountain*.

I'm also fond of "Message to Poets" in *Raids*, and *Eighteen Poems*, the poems he wrote to M, thirteen of which Lynn Szabo includes in the new selected poems, *In the Dark Before Dawn*. I also wouldn't want to be without his essays on Louis Zukofsky and Edwin Muir, nor his translations of Chuang Tzu, and the Nicaraguans Alfonso Cortés and Pablo Antonio Cuadra, the Chilean Nicanor Parra, the Peruvian César Vallejo, nor his satires on Adolf Eichmann.

If I were selecting material for a two-volume edition for The Library of America, in which Merton would take his rightful place between the serenity of Henry David Thoreau and the fire of James Baldwin, the above works, along with key political essays, would constitute the core.

All these works are from the Merton of the sixties, the late Merton, when his bite and merriment, his contemplation and activism, are at their peak. In many ways, Merton belongs to the poets, prophets and protesters of the sixties. His raps on race bring to mind James Baldwin's dialogues with Margaret Mead; his raps on Zen with D.T. Suzuki in New York City connect him to the eastward leanings of Alan Watts, Jack Kerouac and the Beatles. His work on peace and civil rights connect him to Dr. Martin Luther King Jr.

The poet and publisher Lawrence Ferlinghetti seems to intuit Merton's sixties context by including his "Chant to Be Used in Procession Around a Site with Furnaces" in his *Journal for Protection of All Beings*, in company with Bertrand Russell, Norman Mailer and Albert Camus. Merton himself, in his editorship of *Monks Pond*, the journal he begins in the last year of his life, publishes contemporary writers rising to prominence in the sixties: Jack Kerouac, Louis Zukofsky, Wendell Berry and Czeslaw Milosz, among many others.

Sometimes I get by on Merton's sixties writings. Other times, I want everything: all the poems, even the bad ones; all the essays, even the failed ones; all the journals, even the repetitive ones. I have a hundred or so books by and about him in my library. I err on the side of extravagance.

Lawrence S. Cunningham's 1992 selection of Merton's writings, called *Thomas Merton: Spiritual Master*, divides his output into five categories: 1. works where Merton thinks out loud or is being playful, which include his personal journals and letters; 2. works written under holy obedience or from a sense of duty; 3. works "derived from monastic vocation deeply felt and profoundly lived"; 4. literary works, which include his literary essays and his poetry; 5. works celebrating the true self, which includes his main autobiographical work: *The Seven Storey Mountain*, *Jonas*, *Conjectures*, and *The Asian Journal*.

Oddly, Cunningham omits a sixth important category: Merton's social and political writings, which would include the *Cold War Letters*, his letter to Cuadra, and important essays collected in *Passion for Peace*.

In a more recent anthology, *Thomas Merton: Essential Writings*, Christine M. Bochen organizes the Merton canon by a series of calls: the call to contemplation, the call to compassion and the call to unity. The calls entwine and interpenetrate. Bochen includes a significant number of Merton's political poems and selections from his political essays in the calls to both compassion and unity.

I turn to Merton's social and political essays to give myself a reading of the world. The self-defined marginal man clearly sees the centres of power—in the U.S., a snug connection between business, the military and the government—and calls attention to their destruction of society and the environment. Merton remains my chief political weatherman. When I turn to him on politics, the book I rely on is *Passion for Peace: The Social Essays*, edited and with an introduction by Monsignor William H. Shannon.

This book offers Merton's clearest insights into the world's only superpower.

I appreciate three essays from the book in particular: Merton's Swiftian satire, "A Devout Meditation in Memory of Adolf Eichmann"; "War and the Crisis of Language," published posthumously in 1969; and the powerful "The Root of War Is Fear," originally published in *The Catholic Worker* in 1961. This short essay continues to resonate. Jim Wallis's bestseller, *God's Politics*, which offers "a new vision for faith and politics in America," quotes Merton's phrase in Chapter Seven, "Be Not Afraid: A Moral Response to Terrorism." Willis claims on the same page that Jesus' most frequent admonition to his disciples in the New Testament is "Be not afraid." As in Wallis's analysis of war, it seems to me that much of Noam Chomsky's thinking in *Imperial Ambitions: Conversations on the Post-9/11 World* and Michael Moore's thinking in *Fahrenheit 9/11* also piggyback on Merton's diagnosis that war is rooted in fear.

The American historian Howard Zinn recently said on Jon Stewart's late-night talk show that America is addicted to war. Decades earlier, Merton casts the addiction more broadly: "The only possible conclusion is that man is so addicted to war that he cannot possibly deal with his addiction. And yet if he does not learn to cope with it, the addiction will ruin him altogether." The central and prevailing metaphor of American discourse, the word it brings most often to flesh, is war. The war on poverty. The war on drugs. The war on terror.

The United States has a larger military expenditure than Europe, Russia and China combined in order to maintain "725 US military bases in 138 foreign countries." Whatever the problem or crisis, whatever is troubling, the American administration seems to declare war on it. To name a few military interventions since Vietnam, one notes the following: Lebanon. Cuba. Grenada. El Salvador. Nicaragua. Colombia. Chile. Panama. Somalia. Afghanistan. Iraq. To keep this addiction to war going, one needs an enemy, someone who embodies all the scary aspects of one's shadow that one is afraid to face up to.

Merton, decades ahead of his fellow Catholic Michael Moore, diagnoses that the root of war is fear: fear of one's self, fear of the other. As Moore's documentary *Bowling for Columbine* makes clear, particularly in his brilliant animation, his movie-within-the-movie, America has a history of fear. Fear of the Indian. Fear of the black man. Fear of the communist. And now fear of the Muslim.

Fear fuels consumption for corporate profit and justifies governmental violations of privacy. Fear also creates a bogeyman to justify a large corporate-military complex to hunt him and more prisons at home and abroad to house him. The bogeyman changes his face from decade to decade, or even year to year, but he is a constant in the American political imagination. The mightiest nation on earth is the most frightened nation on earth. "Fantasy-based Christian religion," according to New Testament scholar John Dominic Crossan, has "merged steadily and relentlessly with faith-based American foreign policy." Christ's fear-nots have been replaced "with a series of 'fear lots'."

It's not easy to hold Merton's tensions in balance, not easy to honour the knives of his political discourse while also respecting his religious merriment. His politics and prayer would seem to have little in common, and yet, like so much in Merton, they are interconnected.

Prayer, in our time, is a political act. The making of what Merton might call inconsequential sounds that can't be bought or sold on the market, that don't increase one's wealth or status, speaks to the limitations of politics. The sounds or words may come out of the mouth, or remain in the mind, or be expressed bodily. Prayer is the fundamental human posture: the posture of unknowingness, of uncertainty, of nakedness. It is also our natural response to the universe.

"How I pray is breathe," Merton writes in *Day of a Stranger*. He integrates his prayer life into his everyday life:

> It is enough to be, in an ordinary human mode, with one's hunger and sleep, one's cold and warmth, rising and going to bed. Putting on blankets and taking them off, making coffee and then drinking it. Defrosting the refrigerator, reading, meditating, working, praying. I live as my ancestors have lived on this earth, until eventually I die. Amen.

The Toronto sculptor and Catholic layman Ted Rettig sets a context for prayer in our technological and political world in what I regard as the spirit of Merton.

> My prayer life
> is very modest
> and ordinary
> It seems so small
> and unimportant
> so hidden away and ineffectual

not part of our busy world
But I like it very much
and need it
to survive

Ted's prayer has no title, no punctuation, no metaphors. Perhaps it doesn't even conjure any images for the reader, and yet it evokes beauty and wisdom.

In one of his artworks, Ted juxtaposes a photograph of one of his sensuously carved stones with Merton's opening line from "Hagia Sophia": "There is in all visible things an invisible fecundity, a dimmed light, a meek namelessness, a hidden wholeness." Ted's simplicity of image coincides with Merton's simplicity of language against the clutter and babble of the world. He uses Merton for political and prayerful purposes.

Merton has a rich interior life. Robert Lax rhetorically asks in "Harpo's Progress," "How did his work relate to his prayer?" He answers, "The work took its rise from prayer and returned to prayer. The work itself was prayer and was informed by prayer." In Merton's words: "My prayer is then a kind of praise rising up out of the center of Nothing and Silence ... It is not 'thinking about' anything, but a direct seeking of the Face of the Invisible ...."

Merton says these words to his Muslim correspondent Abdul Aziz, who meets Merton on the page, in his writing. He meets the contemplative and activist. That's what the multifaceted Merton offers readers: a meeting and a conversation about prayer and politics.

III

Poet, Reader, Translator

[The poet] seeks above all to put words together in such a way that they exercise a mysterious and vital reactivity among themselves, and so release their secret content of associations to produce in the reader an experience that enriches the depths of his spirit ... Like all great works of art, true poems seem to live by a life entirely their own. What we must seek in a poem is therefore not an accidental reference to something outside itself: we must seek this inner principle of individuality and of life which is its soul ...

—"Poetry, Symbolism and Typology,"
in *Bread in the Wilderness*

Part A: Merton and the Latin American Poets, with an emphasis on Alfonso Cortés

I am completely convinced that without the emergence of an occasional poetic word into consciousness, my monastic life would be fruitless ... I have found by God's grace that other poets, particularly in Latin America (where splendid poetry is being written), have come to be a part of my life and of my monastic vocation too.
—*letter to Father Hans Urs von Balthasar*

P oems. All his life, poems. Towards the end of his life, anti-poems. Earlier: devotional poems, spiritual poems, political poems. Some smooth, others jagged. Praising poems, critical poems. Some, as in his poem on Eichmann, satiric and parodic; others, elegiac. More poems than Yeats, even more than Ginsberg. In many ways, poetry, like prayer, is his natural way of speaking. He writes, reads, teaches and translates poetry.

In a love note, he writes:

I think poetry must
I think it must
Stay open all night
In beautiful cellars

In these jaunty lines, Merton magic-wands instant connections to Hemingway's short story "A Clean Well-Lighted Place" and Edward Hopper's painting *Nighthawks*.

Merton writes poetry in English and French. His poetry ranges from elegies to his brother and Hemingway to found-poems on Eichmann to Zen poetry in *Emblems* to the anti-poetry experiments of *Cables* and *Lograire*. He reads poetry in English, French, Spanish, Portuguese and German, along with the classical languages, Latin and Greek. He lectures on poetry to his novices. He translates poetry, the deepest reading one poet can give another, primarily, though certainly not exclusively, from the Spanish.

In a note on translation, Merton writes: "Translating can be helpful ... Not simply trying to respond more fully to life ... but also technically deepening awareness of the capacity of words, speech, 'idioma' to be real (Octavio Paz). This not only in English but in French, German and Spanish. Particularly Spanish."

His most successful paraphrase-translation is arguably from the Chinese, his *The Way of Chuang Tzu*, with his friend John C.H. Wu's assistance. His engagement with the art of what Thomas Carlyle calls "musical thought" is as complete as any English-speaking poet in the twentieth century. A journal keeper from age sixteen, a monk in his twenties, you can argue that he is a poet from his earliest years in France, when he first begins to name the world bilingually.

Merton's fullest participation with poets and poetry centres on his relationship with the poets and poetry of Latin America. Mostly through extensive letter writing but also, in the case of Ernesto Cardenal, Miguel Grinberg and Nicanor Parra, through personal contact, Merton makes himself intimate with the Spanish poetry of the Americas. He identifies himself as a man of the Americas, an American in the broadest sense, with roots in indigenous Indian cultures, solidarity with African descendants, and deep affection for the Spanish- and Portuguese-speaking peoples of the Americas.

Robert Daggy, in his introductory essay to *Day of a Stranger*, reminds us that Merton wrote his day-journal, the preface to *Obras Completas* (Complete Works), "A Letter to Pablo Antonio Cuadra concerning Giants," "Message to Poets"—written for Miguel Grinberg—"Answers on Art and Freedom" (originally subtitled "for Miguel Grinberg"), "Christian Humanism," "Answers for Hernan Lavin Cerda" (still unpublished in English) and others for South American audiences.

One of the Latin American poets Merton spends time reading and translating is Alfonso Cortés, a Nicaraguan poet who writes extraordinary poetry before falling irretrievably into madness. Merton first mentions reading him in a journal note on March 31, 1965: "A collection of poems [*Poemas Nuevos*] by Alfonso Cortés came, sent by his sister. It looks very interesting. With all his insanity there remains a great wholeness and real penetration in his work, and sometimes a really startling picture of intuition."

Merton seems to have a special relationship with the poets of Nicaragua, that small country which produces magnificent poetry. Nicaraguan Ernesto Cardenal is his novice and close friend. He founds the community of Solentiname, a community for the theology of liberation, spiritual renewal, creative arts, and work with Nicaragua's poor. Pablo Antonio Cuadra, another Nicaraguan whom Merton translates from the Spanish, is the recipient of Merton's incisive analysis of global politics, the famous "A Letter to Pablo Antonio Cuadra Concerning Giants."

In Merton's *Collected Poems*, there are eleven translations of Cortés's poems. His *Emblems of a Season of Fury* contains nine translations plus a poem entitled "To Alfonso Cortés," which acknowledges Cortés's madness—"So droll, to be the mad/Saint of a hot republic!"—but also his victory over the state's ingratitude: "No, you stand still/And you begin to smile/As you read rainbows/On the empty paper." Merton's reading of Latin American poetry is extensive; significantly, forty years after his death, his translations of major Latin American voices are still in use, and in the case of some Cortés's poems are the only published translations in English.

The art of the translator is to juggle two colliding balls: one, be faithful to the original language; and two, write a poem that works in English. Merton successfully transports Cortés's "Great Prayer," for example, from one linguistic home to another.

In Cortés's Spanish, the poem reads:

La gran plegaria
El tiempo es hambre y el espacio es frio
Orad, orad, que sòllo la plegaria
Puede saciar las ansias del vacio.
El sueo es una roca solitaria
En donde el aguila del alma anida:
Sonad, sonad, entre la vida diaria.

In Merton's English, the poem reads:

Great Prayer
Time is hunger, space is cold
Pray, pray, for prayer alone can quiet
The anxieties of void.
Dream is a solitary rock
Where the soul's hawk nests:
Dream, dream, during
Ordinary life

Merton dispenses with the title's definite article, a requirement in Spanish, to make the poem sparer in diction and more metaphysical in vision. He maintains a mythic bareness even when English grammar, like the Spanish, would call for definite articles, as in "the anxieties of the void" over his preferred "the anxieties of void." His other English choice for the Spanish word *vacio* is abyss, but abyss does not strike the note of absolute nothingness as uncompromisingly as void. Notably, too, he chooses to quiet the anxieties of the void rather than to quell them, even though the Spanish may be closer to quell. Anxieties concerning the universe's emptiness are more accurately quieted than quelled.

The Spanish novelist Cervantes admonishes that translation is "like looking at the Flanders tapestries from behind: you can see the basic shapes but they are so filled with threads that you cannot fathom their original lustre." Nevertheless, one feels confident that Merton has made the right linguistic choices in making Cortés's Spanish poem a poem that works in English. There is some loss of lustre. The energy of Spanish is vowel-driven, while the energy in English tends to be consonant-driven. The poem in Spanish has 85 vowels. In English it has 57. One misses the mouthfuls of vowels.

In a May 21, 1965, letter to the Latin American critic and editor Stefan Baciu, Merton outlines a geography of poets in Latin America, from the Nicaraguans Ernesto Cardenal, Pablo Antonio Cuadra and Alfonso Cortés to poets from Ecuador, Chile and Peru. He recognizes his debt to the Spanish poets of the Americas and chastizes North American poets for their "sterile impasse" and their "esoteric tricks of language." He singles out Robert Lowell as an exception and expresses some sympathy for the Beats.

Later, in an August 1, 1966, letter to Baciu, he modifies his "sweeping" and "inconsiderate" generalization in the light of his reading and corresponding with Louis Zukofsky and other American poets. Significantly, Zukofsky is also summoned in Merton's day journal, *Day of a Stranger*, to provide "song" beyond birdsong for his "mental ecology." Merton also calls on the Latin Americans Vallejo and Nicanor Parra, certain European poets, including Rilke, and a good many Chinese "songmakers." Merton informs Baciu that his love affair with Spanish poetry began with his falling "under the spell of F. Garcia Lorca" from which he has never recovered. "He remains," says Merton, "one of my favorite poets and one to whom I respond most completely."

In a letter to poets and translators Rosita and Ludovico Silva on April 10, 1965, Merton writes, "What comes from Mexico, Central America, South America is something to which I can immediately respond. It seems to me a) real and b) civilized." In a line echoing Emily Dickinson's "a Kangaroo among the Beauties," he feels more a part of the Spanish American poetry scene than its North American counterpart where he is "a bramble among the flowers."

Earlier, in a January 8, 1959, letter to Pablo Antonio Cuadra, Merton says very much the same thing: "I am convinced that Latin American poetry has an ambience more pleasing and appropriate for me than that of the United States, which seems a little removed, less spontaneous, less fiery, more cerebral."

Merton's affection for Latin American poets is reciprocated. Ernesto Cardenal, the one-time minister of culture in the Sadinista government, writes poems eulogizing Merton's death. Miguel Grinberg speaks at an international Merton conference in the United States on Merton's "Message to Poets," a manifesto originally written for Grinberg. Stefan Baciu pays tribute to Merton in an American journal.

Baciu, in "The Literary Catalyst," an essay published in *Continuum* shortly after Merton's death, summarizes Merton's contribution to Latin American poets: "During the last two decades, Merton was one of the constant and most accurate spokesmen for this realm [the realm of Latin American poetry] through a series of translations without equal in the literature of the United States, or, for that matter, in world literature." Merton "knew how to love, understand, and interpret the Spanish and Spanish-American worlds," Baciu writes.

He specifically acknowledges Merton's translations of Cortés, Vallejo, Cuadra, and Parra. Baciu concludes his remarks with these words:

> No one like him had been able to contribute to the literature of United States a "living anthology" of the most modern literary movements in Latin America. For this he had the calling, the heart and the knowledge that today almost no one has in this country. With his death the new literature south of the Rio Grande lost not only a friend, but also one of the best and most faithful interpreters.

Certainly Merton shows an astonishing ability to go directly to the spontaneity and fire of a Latin American poet's work in his treatment of Alfonso Cortés:

[Cortés's] idea of "man" (that is of himself) is that of a "mystical tree" on which space and time are fruits produced by the life that is within him: but man's business is not so much to 'comprehend' these fruits of space and time … but rather to live in the full, bewildering and timeless dimension of a life so shattering in its reality that it seems to be madness.

Cortés's is the poetry of cosmology, of stars and planets. In his magic, the outside becomes the inside. There are no separating barriers between within and without, between the stars and the self. What makes the self move and have its being makes the universe move and have its being. This interpenetration is made vivid in Merton's translation of Cortés' poem "Great Prayer."

One of the pleasures of reading Thomas Merton on poetry and poets is to rediscover a familiar voice, such as Louis Zukofsky's, reinterpreted, and to discover a new voice, such as that of Alfonso Cortés, to whom Merton dedicates his poem "Le Secret" with the words "For Don Alfonso Cortés, great poet, with friendship and admiration." About Cortés, Merton further writes:

… Cortés has written some of the most profound "metaphysical" poetry that exists. He is obsessed with the nature of reality, flashing with obscure intuitions of the inexpressible … for he lives in "the origin of things which is not anterior to them, but permanent." This gives his poetry … the strange, unerring certitude of Zen.

Cortés, in "Great Prayer," exclaims without qualification: "Time is hunger, space is cold." He places his poetic hand on how the universe works, how human beings perceive and live within its harsh limits. We have two ways of coping with the hunger and cold. We pray and we dream. There are no sedatives or bromides in Cortés's poem, no false promises or consolations. Cortés does not tell lies. His is the poetry of truth. Merton reads him, translates him, shares his deep-diving into the "ontological sources of life" and makes him as real in English as he is in Spanish.

Part B: Merton and Louis Zukofsky

"Writing to you/Is like writing to my heart/
You are myself."— *Six Night Letters*

Merton offers a detailed reading of the Jewish-American poet Louis Zukofsky in "Louis Zukofsky—the Paradise Ear," one of his most important essays on poetry. Merton recognizes in Zukofsky's poetry, as in "All really valid poetry (poetry that is fully alive and asserts its reality by its power to generate imaginative life) ... a kind of recovery of paradise." The essay is a performance piece where Merton, to a large extent, mimics Zukofsky's child-like idiom in poetry for his own explorative prose. Merton reads and translates Zukofsky into his own experience, in language so close to its source as to blur the line between poet and commentator. He writes about the other as if the other were himself.

The Merton-Zukofsky connection begins with Zukofsky thanking Merton in a letter for his essay. They go on to exchange letters and poems, Zukofsky offering constructive criticism of Merton's poetry and Merton including a page of Zukofsky's writing in *Monks Pond*, Winter, Issue Two in 1968. Through letters and his reading of Zukofsky's poetry, Merton becomes familiar with Zukofsky's wife,

Celia, and son, Paul, both of whom figure prominently in the poetry.

Merton's essay on Zukofsky is originally written in November 1966 and published in *The Critic* in the February–March 1967 issue. He makes one central point in the essay: the poet [Zukofsky] finds "his own way back into Eden" with a "new sound" grounded in "a new start, a new creation." Two months earlier, he had written a long essay on the Orkney poet Edwin Muir entitled "The True Legendary Sound: The Poetry and Criticism of Edwin Muir," and makes a similar point on "the Edenic office of the poet who follows Adam and reverifies the names given to creatures by his first father." Merton sees Muir as "one of those who intuitively realize that the giving of names is a primordial metaphysical act of the human intelligence." Zukofsky, however, is not so much a giver of names as a rememberer of names.

"The business of the poet," Merton writes in his Muir essay, "is to reach the intimate, that is ontological sources of life which cannot be clearly apprehended in themselves by any concept, but which, once intuited can be made accessible to all in symbolic and imaginative celebration." Zukofsky's re-entry into Eden, his recovery of paradise, is through the language of the child in which things are seen and said as if for the first time. Merton compliments Zukofsky on his "inexhaustible, childlike curiosity about words"; he draws attention to his use of words as "chaste and sparing."

According to Merton, Zukofsky "explores all the musical possibilities of ordinary talk about ordinary things" where "Talk is a form of love ...." This talk is also "the essence of conversation with a child" who participates "in the discovery of language, to say words for the first time ...."

Merton gives examples in Zukofsky of Edenic musical thought:

Hello, little leaves
Said not St. Francis
But my son in the spring ...

This child speech, written by an adult, "is paradise speech for it familiarly addresses all things, not yet knowing them as alien and anticipating nothing from them but joy: hence, it is Franciscan." Merton gives two more examples from Zukofsky:

See:
My nose feels better in the air
"Because he was crying

I like him most of all" says my son
"Because he was crying" – the red fox
With three porcupine quills in his paw ...

These poetic snippets emphasize the spoken word; all begin with sound words—"Hello," "See," "Because"—and end with child speech. All are examples of love talk and, in Merton's phrase, Zukofsky's "cosmology of love." The poet "loves his wife and children first, then his relatives and friends, then those he meets."

Zukofsky, Merton maintains, hears and must be heard "with a paradise ear," an ear open to the first stirrings and surges of new life. "His poems in fact cannot be heard except against the vast background of silence and warmth that is the ground and the whole. His poems do not make sense except as part of the whole creation that exists precisely for love, for free, for nothing ...."

Throughout his essay, Merton emphasizes the Blakean Zukofsky, Zukofsky in his songs of innocence, poems that draw their inspiration from a child and seem to be addressed to a child or are voiced by a child. There are other Zukofskys. After all, Zukofsky is the poet who said that one could spend a lifetime delineating the linguistic and metaphysical differences between *a* and *the*. Critic Hugh Kenner, for example, refers to Zukofsky's book-length poem *A* as "the most hermetic poem in English, which they will still be elucidating in the 22nd century." Zukofsky seems to have the mind of a rabbinical scholar, the musicality of a jazz musician, and a sense of fun more common in children than in adults.

He has his songs of innocence, but he also has his songs of experience—jokes, jagged fragments, unpolished haikus, experimental language poems, concrete poems, sound poems, love notes (his famous Valentines to the world) and entangled, incomprehensible utterances that refuse to open to analysis or yield to meaning. Merton gives one such example from the "hermetic" Zukofsky, a poem entitled "And Without."

And without
Spring it is spring why
Is it death here grass somewhere
As dead as lonely walks
As living has less thought that is
The Spring.
Spring it is spring why

Is it death grass somewhere
As dead walks
As living has less thought that is
A spring. And without.

One has a mystery here, and no amount of dissection is going to reduce its inviolable wholeness. If one attempts traditional methods of vivisection, the poem is no longer the poem, but some critical intellectual construct put in its place. Merton dances around the poem, or, if you prefer, embroiders on it, but he does not attempt to trap or cage the poem. "[The poem] cannot be broken down easily into concepts and the poem has to be respected, left alone, only to be read over and over. Then life and death and spring and grass and walking and not-spring and not-thinking-about it, and not-saying-it is spring all become aspects of one unity."

Merton goes on to emphasize the poem's "Zen-likenesses of ordinary life when it might be spring and one is in the midst of a living-dying life in all one's weakness and strength experienced together without contrast, and with no word at hand to signify it, least of all 'spring,' yet it is spring." Spring comes whether we woo it by word or summon it by will, and it comes accompanied by a great many other things. However, even this brief explication of the poem may be too much and unnecessary, for as Merton further testifies, the poem poses a question without provoking an answer that would dispose of it.

The best way to experience the poem is to return to Merton's "Signatures: Notes on the Author's Drawings," published in *Raids on the Unspeakable*. In our context, we can speak of Merton's raids on the non-interpretable. Like

Merton's drawings, Zukofsky's poems "desire nothing but their constitutional freedom from polemic, from apologetic, and from program." They are "simple signs and ciphers of energy ... Their 'meaning' is not to be sought on the level of convention or of concept." Zukofsky's poems, like Merton's drawings, are in Merton's term "inconsequent."

Perhaps the best thing one can do with this particular Zukofsky poem is to hear it, to hear it in its collisions and confusions, in its many-sidedness, in its everything-at-once-ness. Merton captures Zukofsky's playfulness, his odd musicality and his refusal to be easy and immediately comprehensible just as he captures Cortés's spare diction of power and in-seeing.

Ralph Waldo Emerson, says Larzer Ziff in his introduction to the *Penguin* Emerson, "insisted on our reading books only to experience those moments in which we hear a voice that we recognize as proceeding from the same center as our own voices." Merton's close reading of the Latin American Cortés and the Jewish American Zukofsky has to do with their centres being part of his centre, their voices being part of his voice.

IV

Tone Meister

This is simply the voice of a self-questioning human person who, like all his brothers, struggles to cope with turbulent, mysterious, demanding, exciting, frustrating, confused existence in which almost nothing is really predictable, in which most definitions, explanations and justifications become incredible even before they are uttered, in which people suffer together and are sometimes utterly beautiful ...
—Contemplation in a World of Action

A tone meister (or *tonmeister* in German) in the European musical tradition is a sound engineer, a mixer and manipulator of sound. Thomas Merton is a tone meister, a master of tonal subtlety and sculpted sound.

Merton has a way of speaking where, by the magic of his tone, he convinces you that you are a co-writer of his words rather than a mere listener to them. In his best writings, in his most personal confessions, he establishes an extraordinary degree of intimacy between writer and reader. He speaks as friend to friend, as brother to brother.

His August 21, 1967, letter concerning a message of contemplatives to the world enacts the brotherly tone. "We must, before all else, whatever else we do, speak to modern man as his brothers, as people who are in very much the same difficulties as he is, as people who suffer much of what he suffers, though we are immensely privileged to be exempt from so many, so very many, of his responsibilities and sufferings." Nothing pompous here, nothing clever or superior. "[W]e must not arrogate to ourselves the right to talk down to modern man, to dictate to him from a position of supposed eminence ..." he further writes. His is the tone of humility, honesty and solidarity. There is no father or Father voice in middle to late Merton.

As early as *The Sign of Jonas*, Merton is aware of his diverse audiences: "men riding on the Long Island Railroad, nuns in Irish convents, my relatives, secular priests, communists ... and young girls in boarding schools, whom the censors are afraid to scandalize." Whoever or whatever the audience, however large or small the audience, Merton learns to speak intimately to multitudes as if he is speaking to a single person. He learns to speak to the high, middle and low in society because he realizes that everyone, regardless of status or station, lives within the two great biblical metaphors of hunger and thirst.

Science fiction writer, essayist and poet Ursula Le Guin distinguishes between the father voice and the mother voice. Fathers, at least the ones in authority, tend to speak from platforms or lecterns, from heights. They literally speak down to the audience and tend to speak at the audience. Mothers, at least according to Le Guin, tend to speak from a position of equality. They speak in kitchens, in bedrooms, over a cup of coffee or a backyard fence, and are less inclined to pontificate. However, when Mom speaks, she is, in relation to her children at least, in as great a position of authority as Dad is. The metaphor starts to crack.

In his best work, Merton adopts neither the father voice nor the mother voice. He speaks as a sibling, to you as his brother, or to you as his sister. It's a voice you hear in the early masters of American literature. You hear it in both Emerson and Whitman.

I celebrate myself,
And what I assume you shall assume,
For every atom belonging to me as good belongs to you.

These are Whitman's words in *Leaves of Grass*. In the same book, his narrator speaks these lines:

Come closer to me,
Push close my lovers and take the best I possess,
Yield closer and closer and give me the best you possess.

Whitman has an intense and steadfast belief in the democratic equality of each with all.

Emerson also recognizes the magnetic power of personal and intimate words voiced in a tone that knocks down the barrier between the self and the other. In his remarks on Montaigne, he confesses: "It seemed to me as if I had myself written the book, in some former life, so sincerely it spoke to my thought and experience." I've had a similar feeling in reading Merton. I can easily delude myself that if I were as well read and as good a writer as he, I could have written his *Raids, Emblems* or *Seeds*.

In reading Merton, I believe that I am reading a living, struggling human being who is undergoing the same crises and problems that I am facing. His best words are written in the fires of personal experience. One feels called to be a witness to his life. Similarly, Whitman says that whoever touches his book touches a man. The book as flesh. As Emerson says about Montaigne, "Cut these words, and they would bleed; they are vascular and alive." The word as flesh.

Even though at times in Merton one part of himself is speaking to another part—the disciplined self speaking to the wayward self or the monk self speaking to the poet self—the reader as eavesdropper hears the words as if they were spoken from his own lips. A dialogue within the self becomes a dialogue between the self and the other. The reader undergoes the same process of interrogation and criticism as the writer. How this magical transference occurs has to do in part with Merton's tone. The voice as flesh.

Merton gives a great deal of thought to how he sounds. In *Learning to Love*, volume six of his personal journals, he takes to heart a young married woman's response to his essay "Apology to an Unbeliever," and how she has difficulty in hearing God. Merton positions his voice and tone carefully. He mustn't give "an official and 'objective' answer." He must "stand aside from official positions, and speak as a man on her own level" with "no condescension." He mustn't be idolatrous and refuse "to communicate on equal terms." He must use "simple words." He must "try to speak to her as a Brother."

In a subtle and complex letter to Katharine Champney dated November 10, 1966, Merton for the most part lives up to his fierce honesty and strict equality. Towards the end of the letter, he makes clear his quarrel with "religious people" in "the reassurance business" who are "selling answers and consolations." In opposition to such people, Merton says, "I give you no reassurance whatever except that I know your void and I am in it, but I have a different way of understanding myself in it."

Tone is a slippery little word. It's the signature of the voice, the footprint of the tongue. Poets sculpt their individuality by their tones. Rilke, for instance, speaks at times as an angel to a man. One is never sure where the voice is coming from except to know that it falls from a great height and one strains to hear it. *The Duino Elegies* fall with all the magnificence of a Bach fugue. Zukofsky, on the other hand, speaks to us as if we were members of his family. Many of his poems invoke family members, and the reader is temporarily adopted in order to experience the family's joy and anguish.

Tone has to do with how one sounds, whether angry or pompous or flippant. But it also has to do with where one stands when one speaks—whether one is above or below or beside the other. Middle to late Merton speaks friend to friend or brother to sister as if he were standing beside us, on ground neither more nor less elevated than the ground on which we stand. The power of his writing comes, in part, from his standing with us as he speaks, not as an authority or an expert but as a friend who is living through what we are living through as though his life were always co-temporaneous with ours. When Merton condemns his fickleness, for example, we share in the reprimand.

> As soon as you taste one way of prayer, you want to try another. You are always making resolutions and breaking them by counter resolutions. You ask your confessor and do not remember the answers. Before you finish one book, you begin another, and with every book you read you change the whole plan of your interior life. Soon you will have no interior life at all. Your whole existence will be a patchwork of confused desires, and daydreams and velleities in which you do nothing except defeat the work of grace.

He ends the self-flagellation with a pep talk: "So keep still, and let Him do some work." This passage embodies Merton's style of speaking: it is confessional; it is deeply personal; it is intended for himself. But, since it is published, it comes to us as an overheard monologue to which we are privy. The monologue projects beyond itself, reaches for the other, and hence calls us into dialogue. The "you" of the passage is both Merton and ourselves. When one soul opens fully, all souls open a little. He has been so open about his fault that we feel as if it belongs to us as well.

His is the diction of comradeship, the discourse of brotherliness. Merton, in his own phrasing, is "the incarnation of everybody," not as strength but as fragility, not as certainty but as doubt, not as centrality but as marginality. He is aware of this dialectic of identification in which he identifies so closely with us that we are impelled in return to identify with him. In the "Preface to the Japanese Edition of *The Seven Storey Mountain*" he boldly announces, "I seek to speak to you, in some way, as your own self." His tone assumes equality, that his wounds will speak to our wounds. His tone also conveys authority by an odd mixture of audacity and humility.

A fellow Kentuckian, the writer and environmentalist Wendell Berry, on the other hand, sometimes speaks from a hill. We look up to hear him, and he looks down to pronounce. His tone is sometimes teacherly, as demonstrated in his short article on computers in *What Are People For?* which was published earlier to great controversy in *Harper's Magazine*. His tone in poetry is quite different: gentler, quieter, more provisional, less certain.

Berry tells us that computers are a waste of resources, that he prefers the pencil, that his wife types his scripts, that he doubts anyone can demonstrate that a computer has been used to produce work better than Dante's, that he doesn't own a television, that there are certain rules to be learned when determining whether new technology ought to replace old technology. He speaks with authority. He speaks prophetically, perhaps, but he also speaks from higher ground than that which most of us occupy. Here is an example:

A number of people, by now, have told me that I could greatly improve things by buying a computer. My answer is that I am not going to do it. I have several reasons and they are good ones. The first is ... I would hate to think that my work as a writer could not be done without a direct dependence on strip-mined coal. How could I write conscientiously against the rape of nature if I were, in the act of writing, implicated in the rape? For the same reason, it matters to me that my writing is done in the daytime, without electric light.

He goes on to construct a list of eight "shoulds" and one "should not."

The tone is off-putting, even self-righteous, so much so that *Harper's* printed five negative responses in a subsequent issue. Of the twenty letters received, all but three were critical. Readers objected to the implication of impurity or lack of virtue if they persisted in using computers over typewriters or pen and paper. They objected largely to the tone, not the content, of the article, a point missed by Berry in his published reply. Merton, I suspect, would have been at home with computers, but if, for some reason, he rejected them, I suspect that it would be on personal rather than on moral grounds.

To be fair to Berry, his tone can be professorial but also sportive and rich in imagery. Even when his tone misses the mark, his ideas are often so powerful, tightly argued and lived that the message, like a fist, thrusts its way into our life. He writes only when he has something to say. His wisdom, though sometimes lacking in humour, has a homespun quality to it. He writes of particular things, things at his doorstep, in his yard, things that make him happy or sad or angry. If from time to time his tone thunders like Jeremiah, whom he quotes on occasion, the tone is no less legitimate than his tone of celebration, homage or espousal. He has earned his words. His hands have held and felt and worked the soil, the desecration of which he has protested. He has lived by the code of *Ecclesiastes*: "Whatsoever thy hand findeth to do, do it with thy might."

In that loveliest of tracts, *First and Last Memories*, where memory is distilled into art, Brother Patrick Hart recounts his first experience of Merton, then Master of Juniors, leading a gaggle of monks in the planting of loblolly pines. Merton "gave instructions about how they should be planted, heeling them in after one of the novices opened the earth with a spade." Brother Patrick notes that there was little concern for the environment in Kentucky in the early 1950s "except for individuals like Wendell Berry and Thomas Merton."

Wendell Berry writes eloquently about farming, soil, poetry, native peoples, race, the university and language. His poems celebrate the preciousness of everyday encounters with animals and trees and tools. He pays homage to the natural cycles and seasonal changes around his farm in Port Royal on a hillside overlooking the Kentucky River. His essays—works of gratitude to nature, remembrance of friends, and fidelity to place—exhort us to "think small" (the title of one of his finest essays), to attend to the close-at-hand, to care for the soil and vegetation of our region and backyard. The task of world reforestation and global replenishment of depleted topsoil, for instance, is a daunting task, but we can start by planting seedlings, as Merton did, in the small space given to us.

Berry is well acquainted with Merton. He visits Merton at the monastery. He cites Merton as a prophet of wholeness in his essay on nature poetry in *A Secular Pilgrimage*. In his essay "Discipline and Hope," he closes with a Merton anecdote. Merton was once asked why the Shakers, who expected the end of the world at any moment, were nevertheless consummate farmers and craftsmen. He replied that when you expect the world to end at any moment, you know there is no need to rush. You take your time, and you do your work well.

The tone of early Merton, pre–*Sign of Jonas*, say, can be stiffer and more dogmatic than anything in Berry. But the tone Merton strikes in one of his last talks, an informal address given in Calcutta just days before his death in Bangkok, displays the humour, self-deprecation, understatement and festivity associated with middle to late Merton. He begins the talk by poking fun at his clerical collar, noting that his usual costume is blue jeans and open shirt. He reassures the audience that he is supposed to be a monk, although he may not look like one. He then identifies himself as a marginal person in league with poets and hippies. As in the *New Seeds* passage quoted earlier, he uses the second person plural, establishes an I-you relationship and maintains an I-you dialogue.

> So I ask you to do me just the favor of considering me not as a figure representing any institution but as a statusless person, an insignificant person who comes to you asking your charity and patience while I say one or two things that have nothing to do with my [prepared] paper.

His tone here is playful and intimate, a brother joking with a sister.

Berry, on the other hand, in his article on computers, badgers. He seems elevated and distant. He speaks as a minister to a congregation, a master to an apprentice or a father to a child. He seems wiser and more hardworking and more committed to the right causes than we are. In contrast, Merton seems acutely aware of his own shortcomings.

The messages of Merton and Berry, couched in Berry's magical phrasing, are ultimately the same: "To keep oneself fully alive in the Creation, to keep the Creation fully alive in oneself, to see the Creation anew, to welcome one's part in it anew." The manner in which the messages are communicated occasionally differs. Tone may not directly affect the meaning of the words, but it does affect the likelihood of our listening to, and acting on, the words.

V

Letter Writer

Write what is deepest in your heart ...
—*Thomas Merton, in a letter*

Some write good letters. Others don't. My father wrote warm, personal letters full of encouragement. The letter was an art form at which he excelled and in which he seemed at ease. He always wrote as an equal to the person he was addressing. My personal library contains numerous volumes that he bequeathed to me, including a number of volumes by Merton with underlined or starred passages. I follow Dad's mind by tracking the places where his fingers stop to comment or star. He continues to light my way.

The Merton books that he bought me or read at my urging frequently come with letter-like inscriptions, as in his words in the inside cover of *Bread in the Wilderness*: "You appear to have been captivated by the scholarly and spiritual character of this man. Walk with him gently and prayerfully. You will be richly rewarded. Thank you for all the joy and love I have known and shared as we journeyed together. Sincerely and gratefully, Dad—Christmas 88." He writes these words a few years before the fog of Alzheimer's begins to envelop his mind.

My wife, mother and sister write wonderfully detailed letters full of observations on their lives and surroundings. They feel comfortable in the form. I feel awkward. Most of the time I don't feel like talking. I resist the letter's call, and when I finally succumb to it, I resent the letter for forcing me to talk. Something of that tension and unresolved conflict seeps into my correspondence, I'm sure.

My son and daughter are zappers. They zap their friends with e-mails, quick jolts of presence and good wishes. Like them, I'm more comfortable in the quick electricity of an e-mail than the measured and considered thought of a letter.

Sometimes the famous also seem to be uncomfortable in the letter. They give you the feeling that they'd rather be writing something else. Skip Hemingway's letters unless you enjoy someone carping page after page on the shortage of money or the blindness of critics. Skip Dylan Thomas's letters unless money and booze are subjects of great interest. The best letter writers—St. Paul, Keats, Chekhov, Van Gogh—carve out a place in literature by the quality of their words and the urgency with which they express them. While not a Paul or a Keats in the letter form—who is?—Merton is a very good letter writer and incredibly prolific. He churns out letters the way a hen lays eggs, effortlessly and unceremoniously.

Dr. Zilboorg, Merton's monastically assigned psychiatrist, finds him "verbological." An incessant babbler. He wants to take Merton off words the way a detox counsellor wants to take an alcoholic off booze. Says he could only be alone in New York City. Only quiet in Grand Central Station with a sign above his begging bowl and blanket proclaiming "Hermit lives here."

The criticism seems excessive, but it does contain an element of truth. A man who is supposed to be silent for the most part impishly finds creative ways of talking. Talk—what Merton sometimes calls "a vow of conversation"—is as central to his being as his silence, solitude and study. Blame it on his Welsh genes, perhaps. Welsh on both his mother's (Jenkins) and father's side. Blame it on his Irish as well. I like to recall Brother Patrick Hart's comment that one of the last things Merton was working on before his death was the Irish language. The gab of pub-formed cultures has a special place in the world's singing.

At any rate, Merton is a compulsive writer and letter writer, a word addict, as driven to put word on page as Dostoevsky was driven to roll the dice. He jokes to a nun, Anne Saword, that people think he secretes articles like perspiration. He admits to Abbot James Fox, also in a jocular tone, that if he were forbidden to write, he'd end up in a mental hospital. Merton seems at home in language, and at ease in all forms of writing, especially the epistolary form. It is, after all, the means by which he maintains his old friendships from his student days at Columbia, and acquires newer, more virtual friendships. Merton scholar William H. Shannon enlightens us that "there are some 3,500 letters addressed to well over a thousand correspondents" at the Thomas Merton Studies Center at Bellarmine University in Louisville, Kentucky.

Merton writes to "poets and heads of states; to popes, bishops, priests, religious and lay people; to monks, rabbis, and Zen masters; to Catholics, Protestants, Anglicans, Orthodox Christians, and Jews; to Buddhists, Hindus, and Sufis; to literary agents and publishers; to theologians and social activists; to old friends and young ones, too."

His content is as diverse as his audience.

Merton writes about Allah, Anglicanism, Asia, the Bible, the Blessed Virgin, Buddhism, China, Christ, Christendom, Church, conscience, contemplation, and the cold war; about Eckhart, ecumenism, God, happiness, his hermitage, and his hospital interludes; about illusions, Islam, John of the Cross, Julian of Norwich, Martin Luther King, Jr., the Koran, Latin America, liturgy, the love of God, poetry, political tyranny, precursors of Christ, prophets, psalms, silence, solitude and *sobornost*; about technology, Trinity, unity, the will of God, his own writings.

I enjoy Monsignor Shannon's list, but I'm also inclined to add a few other Merton topics: beer, art, dreams, books, Bob Dylan, Joan Baez, mountains, trees, peace, war, dance, jazz, laughter and so on.

Nowhere is Merton more relaxed and easier with words than in his correspondence with Robert Lax, the man who writes skinny poems. No friend or critic sees Merton more clearly or more holistically than Lax. His "Harpo's Progress," his "Remembering Thomas Merton in New York," his journal jottings about Merton, and his letters exchanged with Merton are unparalleled in their intimacy, love and understanding. Theirs is one of the deepest literary friendships of the twentieth century.

Their letters read like e-mails. Two boys on the playground of the page toss Frisbees back and forth, each one trying to go a little higher or shine a little brighter. The letters tickle and tease. They're Merton's cables to the world, and in the Lax correspondence, they are how he maintains his friendship with his closest friend. Once Merton enters the monastery, Lax's visits become less frequent, and when Lax goes to live on the island of Patmos, Greece, personal contact stops altogether. Lax is in Patmos when he hears the news that Merton will not be able to fulfill his planned visit to the island.

As if taking on new identities, much as e-mailists do now, Merton signed off his letters to friend Ed Rice with a range of complimentary closes: Uncle O'Remus, Roosevelt, Homer, Wang, Joey Zimmerman, Nestles, Inc.,

Happy, Joey the Chocolate King, Jess Stacey, Llwellen, Frisco Jack, Alban Leixos, Marco J. Frisbee. With Rice, if only for a page or two, Merton could be a Greek, a Jew, Chinese, a poet, a president, a corporation, a flying disk and a boy. With Lax, he strikes other poses, including Harpo, which Lax makes use of in his brilliant summary of Merton's life and work in "Harpo's Progress." Within these masks, identities are fluid, changeable, even interchangeable. They're subject to mood and chance.

Merton and Lax develop a kind of private language reminiscent of Jonathan Swift's baby talk in *Journal to Stella* and perhaps James Joyce's freewheeling letters to his wife, Nora. Here is an example from Merton's February 24, 1965, letter to Lax:

> Dear Most
> Wabes have brought me yours numerous with syllabo i will think i will think … I have wrotten you a proverb in plaint of fact with sybbalo. Sy-lla-bule.

No topic seems off limits, as in Merton's letter to Lax dated October 5, 1963, on his medical condition:

> Was in the hospital again, all the same old things, cut, shot, bruised, battered, pasted, kneaded, heated, peeled, swept, chilled, fed, overfed, glutted, soaked, chopped and thrown back to the winter weeds of Nelson hills.

In his implied metaphoric fireworks, Merton is kneaded like bread, peeled like an onion, swept like a floor, chilled like wine, and soaked like dirty laundry.

In the same letter, Merton spoofs his recent work in calligraphy:

Me and Ad Reinhardt [F] have been carrying on correspondence by obscure telepathies and hidden calligraphic
paintings of which I must tell Charlie I got ten million. I
make the fastest calligraphic paintings in the world, twenty
nine a second, zip zip zip all over Kentucky they fly in the
air the doves bear them away to no galleries. My art is pure
I tell you it is pure. Like I said got swarms of calligraphies
the only thing wrong with them says Ad is they too small,
only about a foot long, real calligraphies got to be so vast you
can't get them out of the building.

As a footnote, I should add that Reinhardt sends
Merton proper paper for his calligraphies, and arranges
for his friend Ulfert Wilkie to give him some coaching in
calligraphy.

Merton and Lax constantly encourage each other in
their correspondence. They take a keen interest in each
other's work, and they see each other's work in startling
clarity. In Lax's October 12, 1963, letter, he exhorts his
friend to produce more art, visual and linguistic, and he
sees the interconnectedness of everything he does:

> write more poems and make more calligraphies:
> the poems help the calligraphies, the calligraphies
> help the poems; the poems and the calligraphies
> help the manifestos; you will see, you will see.

Lax's use of the verb *help* is interesting here. Merton's
worlds—the spiritual, the artistic, the poetic and the political—entwine and draw strength from each other. Each
part of his production helps us to see the whole.

Merton is free to speak his mind to Lax. You see that
clearly in Merton's November 10, 1963, letter where he

mocks the censors of the Church and the Order under whose watchful eyes he is forced to write. In mid-letter, Merton starts playing with his "thaumastic typewriter," trying out a range of accents on the vowels *e*, *a* and *o*. Into his merriment, he inserts a barb or two aimed at the censors:

> ... (for the censors a little caca, otherwise they would be duped and hoaxed.) ... (for the censors a little cocu, how they ever going to do any business if there is no cocu in the manuscript?)

And on the zaniness goes. Merton's and Lax's *A Catch of Anti-Letters* is unique in Merton's epistolary history. Publishers have recently published separate books of Merton's letters with writers—with the poet Milosz, his publisher James Laughlin, and theologians Rosemary Ruether and Jean Leclerq, etc.—but no collection has the spontaneity and silliness of two men allowing themselves to be boys with each other.

When not writing to friends, Merton tends to be more serious in tone and subject matter. In contrast to his easy, light manner with friends and children, his correspondence with Rosemary Ruether reveals another side. He's self-conscious, defensive, nervous. Ruether is more woman than he bargained for. She's strong, opinionated, tough-minded. She shows him no deference, unlike the nuns and mothers and female guests who visit him. When he accuses her of being too cerebral, she jumps back at him with full weight. If you like sparks and fireworks, the Merton-Ruether correspondence is hard to beat.

She seems to get the better of him, although I recall her words years ago at Five Oaks, a United Church retreat centre in southern Ontario, that one of the things she took away from Merton years after the correspondence was a heightened sense of the sacramental vision. I haven't read her theology closely in recent years, but what little I have read confirms that she has moved towards greater appreciation of liturgy and sacrament. Still feisty, still a champion of the world's underdogs, but more open to the non-utilitarian.

What Merton may have taken from her in the correspondence is a less idealized view of women. To his credit, Merton doesn't speak down to her or try to pull rank; he sounds defensive of his monastic vocation, and perhaps overly self-conscious of her being a woman, but he never sounds paternalistic or superior. In a preface written almost twenty years after their correspondence, Ruether writes:

> What comes across in these letters is that, although we were separated by more than twenty years in age, he as a seasoned thinker and I as a neophyte, Merton from the beginning addressed me as an equal ... Occasionally he assumed the stance of subordinate, asking me to be his teacher or even confessor. But never did he take the paternalistic stance as the father addressing the child, which is more typical of the cleric, especially in relation to women. Mostly in these letters, we dialogue and even scrap with each other as intellectual siblings.

Her phrase "Merton from the beginning addressed me as an equal" has particular resonance for me. It's the tone my father always used in his letters to me, even when I was a child.

Aside from the Lax correspondence, another time when Merton is conspicuously at ease in his correspondence is with a sixteen-year-old high school student, Suzanne Butorovich. She writes from California to ask him to make a contribution to her school's underground newspaper. In his June 22, 1967, letter to the girl, Merton begins by saying, "I like underground movements and publications, they are irresistible." He sends her "Prayer to the Computer" from *Cables to the Ace*. He tells her that the long, fragmented poem sounds a bit like Bob Dylan. He says for her to go ahead and educate him musically even though he's not completely in a time warp. He knows who Paul McCartney is and he has the Beatles album *Revolver*. He ends the letter by saying, "... I love the hippies and am an underground hippy monk but I don't need LSD to turn on either. The birds turn me on."

Merton continues the banter, a playful uncle talking to a clever niece, until his preparations for his Asian trip. In one of her letters to Merton, Suzanne kisses the page, leaving a red lip mark. Merton responds by thanking her "for the beautiful engraving in red," and adds, "I don't know what to do about that one. Maybe I could give you a footprint of my head." In his next letter, he tells her that he has written a poem called "Why I Have a Wet Footprint on Top of My Mind."

In his letters to Suzanne Butorovich, Merton follows his own advice given in a November 4, 1965, letter to a young, aspiring Dublin writer, John O'Keefe. In paraphrase, Merton says:

Don't talk down to anyone.
Don't just tell people what they want to hear.
Write "what is deepest in your own heart."
Write only what you've thoroughly learned ...

The first point in particular is much in evidence. Merton writes to Suzanne as an equal. He asks her for advice, for recommendations; he empathizes and encourages.

Occasionally, Merton seems to lose himself in his own poetry. When writing to a sixth-grader, Susan Chapulis from Connecticut, he seems to go beyond satisfying the simple request for information on "Monks and Monasteries." He grants that monks can be a little crazy, going off by themselves, and then adds this poetic sentence:

On the other hand when you are quiet and when you are free from a lot of cares, when you don't have to worry about your car and your house and all that, and when you don't make enough money to pay taxes, and don't have a wife to fight with, and when your heart is quiet, you suddenly realize that everything is extremely beautiful and that just by being quiet you can almost sense that God is right there not only with you but even in you.

One suspects that this is more information than a sixth-grader needed. Nevertheless, the words are what is deepest in Merton's heart and what he knows thoroughly.

One is struck in the complete correspondence by how frequently Merton discloses secrets to strangers. To Boris Pasternak, he reveals his fantasy life; to a Sufi scholar, his working day; to a Dubliner, his standards for writing; and to a girl in grade six, some of his deepest convictions concerning monastic life.

Of all the many volumes of letters, the one that speaks to me most personally is the volume reserved for writers. It's called *The Courage for Truth* and it contains most of his letters to writers, although not the ones to Lax or Mark Van Doren and not the ones surrounding his editorship of the literary journal *Monks Pond*. Two of the high marks of this collection include the letters to two giants of twentieth-century poetry, Boris Pasternak and Czeslaw Milosz.

The correspondence with Milosz sometimes gets entertainingly combative. Milosz isn't enamoured of the American peace movement nor of Merton's involvement in it; he chides Merton's idealized view of nature; he nips at some of the modernist tendencies of the Catholic Church. In his way, he is as combative as Ruether. Merton takes all this fencing in stride, reminding Milosz, who fears he may have wounded the monk, that "There was nothing wounding in your letter. Anything you may be tempted to think about the Church, I think myself, and much more so as I am in constant contact with all of it."

The tone with Milosz is direct, warm and playful. With Pasternak, Merton adopts a more reverential tone. He knows that he is writing to a great figure in modern literature. And yet, despite the reverence, he intimately reveals a dream narrative about a young girl whom he calls Proverb:

> One night I dreamt I was sitting with a very young Jewish girl of fourteen or fifteen, and that she suddenly manifested a very deep and pure affection for me and embraced me so that I was moved to the depths of my soul ... I spoke to her of her name [Proverb], and she did not seem to be proud of it, because it seemed that the other young girls mocked her

for it. But I told her that it was a very beautiful name, and there the dream ended.

One is a little surprised that a monk can so casually let a stranger into his dream life, even into what Jungian psychology would term his anima. The dream of Proverb also triggers one of Denise Levertov's great poems, "I learned that her name was Proverb."

Merton also shares a good deal of himself with Latin American writers, in contrast to the reticence he maintains with American writers. He seems to feel more at home when he is away from home and more at ease with foreigners than with fellow Americans. His Latin letters tend to be exuberant and celebratory, while his American letters lean towards the laconic and the emotionally restrained. The exceptions are his skylarking with Henry Miller and his bouncy correspondence with Lawrence Ferlinghetti.

The correspondence with the Latins seems wonderfully relaxed and informal. To Miguel Grinberg, he writes: "I am in my fiftieth skin and trying to get it off like a tight bathing suit, too wet, too sticky, and irritating in the extreme." As he does so often, Merton says profound things in a playful manner. He spoofs in the same letter to Grinberg: "No hermit is important. That is why hermits are essential in a universe that is being ruined by a plague of important people. Down with importance. Down with the importance of monks ...."

In the letters to Latin American writers, the reader at times wants to break into the narrative and interrogate the monk. Such a moment occurs in his letter to Pablo Antonio Cuadra, the Nicaraguan poet he translates and whom he honours in an essay called "A Letter to Pablo Antonio Cuadra Concerning Giants":

> We have a tremendous ... vocation, the vocation of being Americans, ... of being and of forming the true America that is the Christ of the Americans: the Christ that was born among the Indians already many centuries ago, who manifested himself in the Indian culture, before the coming of official Christianity: the Christ that has been crucified for centuries on the great cross of our double continent; the Christ that is agonizing on this same cross; when will the hour of the Resurrection of our Christ of the Americas come?

Would that Merton had had the time and the inclination to flesh out this brief passage in more detail. As the passage stands, it tantalizes the reader with a fresh and radical understanding of Christology, and hints at the beginnings of a new appreciation of Native spiritual traditions.

All his adult life, Merton regards himself as a man of the Americas, the complete Americas, the south as well as the north, the Spanish as well as the Anglo. The Indian roots of the Americas are the unifying factor, that which brings both sides of the divide together, along with a continental commitment to Christ. Merton's Christ is not confined to Jesus of Nazareth and Judea, the Christ of a particular dot in time; Christ resides outside of time and place, in each time and place. Merton is interested in "the Christ of the ikons," "the Christ of immediate experience all down through the mystical tradition." Not knowledge of Christ as a particular Jewish mystic, but knowledge *in*

Christ. "Christ not as object of seeing or study, but Christ as center in whom and by whom one is illuminated."

Letters to Ernesto Cardenal, Jacques Maritain, Evelyn Waugh and Louis Zukofsky one also reads with profit and delight. One thing remains clear throughout: Merton the poet is always at the same time Merton the monk. The poet writes from the monk's deep spiritual resources, and the monk writes with the poet's craft and love of language. When Merton puts his fingers on the typewriter, it is frequently, like Pasternak, with whom he felt such kinship, to advance the cause of the Spirit in "an age of deep spiritual winter." He writes not to advance his own name among poets—he seldom talks about his poetry except to ask for criticism—but to recharge the creative and spiritual energies within himself, within his correspondents, and ultimately within his readers, happy eavesdroppers to his wit and wisdom.

VI

Public Intellectual

If I dare, in these few words, to ask you some direct and personal questions, it is because I address them as much to myself as
to you. It is because I am still able to hope that a civil exchange
of ideas can take place between two persons—that we have not
yet reached the stage where we are all hermetically sealed, each
one in the collective arrogance and despair of his own herd.
—"Letter to an Innocent Bystander," in *Raids on the Unspeakable*

Part A: Columbia University's Heritage and Legacy:
Merton & Edward Said

"I am on the side of the people who are being burned, cut to pieces, tortured, held as hostages, gassed, ruined, destroyed."
—*Faith and Violence*

Bookman and linguist George Steiner playfully defines an intellectual as a reader with a pencil. By such definition, Thomas Merton, a man frequently at book and at scribble, is undoubtedly an intellectual.

If an intellectual is a reader with a pencil, a public intellectual is someone who takes his pencil and paper to the street. He attempts to address a large audience about matters of urgency. By such definition, Thomas Merton is a public intellectual.

Intellectual is not a word Merton disavows. In "Letter to an Innocent Bystander," an important essay in *Raids on the Unspeakable*, Merton writes:

But who are "we"? We are the intellectuals who have taken for granted that we could be "bystanders" and that our quality as detached observers could preserve our innocence and relieve us of responsibility. By intellectual, I do not mean clerk … I do not mean bureaucrat. I do not mean politician. I do not mean technician. I do not mean anyone whose intelligence ministers to a machine for counting, classifying and distributing other people: who hands out to this one a higher pay check and to that one a trip … I do not mean a policeman, or a propagandist. I still dare to use the word intellectual as if it had a meaning.

Merton's social and political network is broad and deep. He befriends the socialist Nicaraguan Ernesto Cardenal, publishes in such left-leaning journals as *Ramparts* and *The Catholic Worker*, has strong ties to the peace movement, and speaks out in the *Cold War Letters* and elsewhere against the Military-Industrial Complex of his day. He wants to be read, and he is. He wants to speak to a broad public, and he does so.

Merton, who completes his undergraduate and graduate degrees at Columbia University in New York City, hails from a long line of Columbian public intellectuals—from Mark Van Doren, Lionel Trilling and Jacques Barzun in his own day to Gayatri Spivak and Edward Said in more recent times—most of whom are noted for critique and dissent. Before, during and after the Merton years at Columbia, the university is, in Barzun's phrase, a "House of the Intellect." Heir to a legacy of enlightened humanism, Merton writes for the general reading public rather than the select priests and initiates of a given discipline.

Like Saint Augustine, he is turned around by his reading. With Augustine, the turnaround comes from Cicero, the Platonists and Saint Paul. With Merton, the turnaround comes from his studies at Columbia University.

In 1937, as noted by Robert Inchausti in *Thomas Merton's American Prophecy*, Merton reads Étienne Gilson's *The Spirit of Medieval Philosophy* and Aldous Huxley's *Ends and Means*. On the suggestion of the Hindu monk Brachmachari, who was teaching at Columbia at the time, he reads Saint Augustine's *Confessions* and Thomas à Kempis's *Imitation of Christ*. He later picks up Jacques Maritain's *Art and Scholasticism*. He immerses himself

in William Blake. He reorients himself through his reading; book-words acquire spirit. Later, to paraphrase Saint
Teresa, "Words lead to deeds ... they prepare the soul,
make it ready, and move it to tenderness."

Merton's own incomparable way of speaking of his literary conversion to Christian thought is to say, "I ended up
by being turned on like a pinball machine by Blake, Thomas
Aquinas, Augustine, Eckhart, Coomaraswamy, Traherne,
Hopkins"—about whom he wished to do his doctorate—
"Maritain and the sacraments of the Catholic Church." His
Columbian years contrast sharply with the desultory years
at Cambridge. At Columbia, as a secular man, he upholds a
religious tradition of reading as a spiritual practice, reading
as a potentially transformative experience.

Another part of his Columbian heritage is political
engagement. Merton reorients himself again in 1961. He
turns to systematic political analysis for the first time. The
self and the sacraments, two of his large themes until this
pivotal date, are not enough. As previously quoted, his
August 23, 1961, letter to Catholic activist Dorothy Day
announces a new direction for his writing: "I don't feel
that I can in conscience ... go on writing just about things
like meditation ... I cannot just bury my head in a lot of
rather tiny and secondary monastic studies either. I think
I have to face the big issues, the life-and-death issues."
"Love," to use poet Richard Wilbur's paraphrase of Saint
Augustine, "Calls Us to the Things of This World." Love
brings Merton into the political area. One fights for what
one loves.

As noted by William Shannon, in the summer of 1961
Merton writes three of his most famous political tracts:

his "Auschwitz poem," better known as "Chant to Be Used in Processions around a Site with Furnaces," the documentary satire "Original Child Bomb" (on the American nuclear devastation of Hiroshima and Nagasaki), and his "Letter to Pablo Antonio Cuadra Concerning Giants," an evisceration of American and Soviet foreign and domestic policies. These works display his knives without the merry mind. Muted rage in these tracts speaks to the desecration of life and human beings, and the soiling of the sacred.

These works rebel against the manipulation and destruction of innocents, the large Orwellian boot on the human face. These works lay the ground for Merton's subsequent analysis of war and peace in his 111 *Cold War Letters*, the political work he manages to mimeograph and send to friends despite his monastery's censorship and ban on such activities.

His teacher and fellow Columbian Mark Van Doren says he never experienced an intellectual with a mind "more brilliant, more beautiful, more serious, more playful" than Merton's. The brillance, the beauty, the seriousness and the play reside in his politics and poetry, in his contemplation and calls to action. Call Thomas Merton, then, an intellectual with a cassock, an intellectual with knives, a monk in whom impish levity co-exists with a penchant for gravitas and intellectual debate.

When social critic Morris Berman in *The Twilight of American Culture* talks about "the monastic option" as a way of addressing "our contemporary cultural crisis," it's difficult not to think that he may have someone like Thomas Merton in mind. When Berman writes of today's new "monk" bent on resisting "the spin and hype of the global corporate world order" and as someone who knows "the difference between reality and theme parks, integrity and commercial promotion," one thinks of a certain Trappist who died in Bangkok in 1968.

According to Berman, the "new monk," for which he even coins an acronym, "NMI, new monastic individual," is "a sacred/secular humanist, dedicated not to slogans or the fashionable patois of postmodernism, but to Enlightenment values that lie at the heart of our civilization: the disinterested pursuit of the truth, the cultivation of art, the commitment to critical thinking ...." Merton would also want to add that the intellectual must commit to "Gospel-inspired social action."

What does a monk offer the world? Praise. Silence. Solitude. Ritual. Prayer. What does a Zorba monk like Merton additionally offer the world? Realness. Vision. Understanding. Solidarity. Struggle. The monk lives out another way of being human, another way of connecting to heaven and earth. An articulated life on the margins, truly lived and expressed as Merton's life was, potentially enables everyone in society to see the centre more clearly, to see who benefits from power—corporate and governmental—and who is at its mercy. The Court Jester knows the workings of the Kingdom; the marginal monk knows the nature of power and how it is exercised. The monk also knows there are more things present and alive in the universe than the ching of the money machine.

In recent decades, the legacy of Columbia's intellectual heritage passed to the late Edward W. Said, Parr Professor of English and Comparative Literature. Said, a Palestinian activist and scholar of literature and music with an international reputation, defines the intellectual in his *Representations of the Intellectual* much more fully than Morris Berman's teasing probe and George Steiner's sportive remark. For Said, the intellectual's job is to:

> … question patriotic nationalism, corporate thinking, and a sense of class, racial or gender privilege.

> … this role has an edge to it, and cannot be played without a sense of being someone whose place it is publicly to raise embarrassing questions, to confront orthodoxy and dogma … to be someone who cannot easily be co-opted by governments or corporations …

The intellectual belongs on the same side with the weak and unrepresented. The intellectual is always "a traveler, a provisional guest, not a freeloader, conqueror, or raider."

> The intellectual in exile is necessarily ironic, skeptical, even playful—but not cynical.

> Exile means that you are always going to be marginal, and that what you do as an intellectual has to be made up because you cannot follow a prescribed path.

In these last few quotations, one can be forgiven for thinking that Thomas Merton is speaking, so Mertonian is Said's talk of exile, playfulness and marginality.

Said goes on in his book-length essay to spell out specific qualities of the intellectual. He must not be beholden to a power centre: the corporation, the government or the university; he must as far as possible avoid slavish specialization; he must be an amateur, in its root sense of being a lover, a lover of truth, even if it collides with sacred or official texts. To be a "Saidean" intellectual one must be "a thinking and concerned member of a society … entitled to raise moral issues at the heart of even the most technical and professionalized activity …."

If one goes through Said's extended definition of the intellectual—including responsibilities, function, and moral stance—one finds how accurately it matches the intellectual life of Thomas Merton. Merton is the man in exile from a one-dimensional technological society, the man without an agenda, the man on the margins, someone who is neither on governmental nor corporate payroll. The moneyed classes may expect monks, particularly Trappist ones, to keep their mouths shut, but Merton seldom lives according to the expectations of the financially and politically or ecclesiastically powerful. He is *l'homme engagé*.

Throughout the sixties, Merton rages vociferously in books, articles and letters against the Vietnam War, racism, the Cold War and the threat of nuclear war, against the trampling of indigenous peoples, the all-pervasive power of the corporation in its advertising and its links to the military, and against the technologizing of society and the individual. His analysis of Vietnam is particularly striking.

He asks himself what power propels "the massive stupidity," then answers: "It is the obsession of the American mind with the myth of know-how, and with the capacity to be omnipotent." Once this myth is questioned, Merton goes on, "we will go to any lengths … to resolve the doubt that has been raised in our minds." Merton then points to Vietnam as the learning ground of "how bestial and how incredible are the real components of the myth." He finishes his thought with this pellucid insight: "Vietnam is the psychoanalysis of the U.S."

Merton's intellectual mission seems similar to Jonathan Swift's, as articulated by Edward Said in "Swift as Intellectual" in *The World, the Text and the Critic*. It's concerned with "organized human aggression or organized human violence": "conquest, colonial oppression, religious factionalism, the manipulation of minds and bodies, schemes for projecting power on human beings, and on history, the tyranny of the majority, monetary profit for its own sake, the victimization of the poor by a privileged oligarchy."

The two political agendas, one in the eighteenth century and the other in the twentieth, speak out against entrenched and co-opting power. Merton, in his last public address in Bangkok, "Marxism and Monastic Perspectives," thunders: "The monk is essentially someone who takes up a critical attitude towards the world and its structures ... the monk is somebody who says, in one way or another, that the claims of the world are fraudulent."

Merton resists the prevailing conformities and orthodoxies of the time. He mounts his sixties attack by way of two distinct verbal strategies: his meditational works emphasize the interior life of thoughtfulness and self-criticism as an antidote to a life of frenzied consumption and the cult of things; and his political and social writings make use of what Kierkegaard calls "the negative way," the use of satire, irony and parody as a way of uncovering the deceptions and seductions of what Neil Postman, a public intellectual and communications theorist not from Columbia, calls "technopoly": a society that is not only governed by technological concerns, but also a society whose highest aspirations fall within a technological sphere.

In simple English, technopoly has to do with the production of wealth made possible by business computers and the protection of that wealth by military-computer technologies. In a society in which the technological way of being has a monopoly on the expression of the human— in other words, in a technopoly—what makes money and what protects it makes the only rational sense. In such a society, the monk, in his refusal to worship dollars or success, presents a radically alternative way of being in the world.

Part B: Mind at Work: Merton & Adolf Eichmann

"Your world is full of me, I am all over the place, I am legion."
— *Conjectures of a Guilty Bystander*

Thomas Merton exercises his Columbia-shaped mind on a number of key social and political issues. He writes cogently on war and peace, the black revolution, technology, and indigenous cultures. He also has a great deal to say on the misuse and brutality of power. These political writings, not just his monastic writings, justify Robert Lax's phrase: *hermit at the heart of things*.

Merton sees the menace of the Nazis early and clearly. In a cartoon of a party in 1938, he draws a swastika on a male partygoer's shoulder. In 1941, he writes his novel "Journal of My Escape from the Nazis," which is eventually published as *My Argument with the Gestapo*. In his

Author's Preface written in 1968, he recalls a firsthand experience of the Nazi callous disregard for human life. It's Sunday morning, in the spring of 1932. Merton is hiking through the Rhine Valley near Koblenz. A fast-moving car jammed with people suddenly appears.

> Almost before I had taken full notice of it, I realized it was coming straight at me and instinctively jumped into the ditch. The car passed in a cloud of leaflets and from the ditch I glimpsed its occupants, six or seven youths screaming and shaking their fists. They were Nazis, and it was election day. I was being invited to vote for Hitler, who was not yet in power. These were future officers in the SS. They vanished quickly. The road was once again perfectly silent and peaceful. But it was not the same road as before. It was now a road on which seven men had expressed their readiness to destroy me.

The individual Nazi whom Merton writes most about is Adolf Eichmann. Was he one of the boys in the car? Merton marshalls all his linguistic and artistic resources to paint one of the most searing portraits of a Nazi officer on record. He draws knives from his normally merry mind.

Born in Solingen, Germany, on March 19, 1906, Adolf Eichmann, the son of an accountant and a religious Protestant family, was married with four sons. Known by fellow Nazis as "the Jewish specialist," he was a German nationalist, an ambitious party member, and "the face of Nazi mass murder." In the English historian David Cesarani's recent comprehensive biography, Eichmann is the consummate manager who organizes genocide "in the way that the director of a multi-national corporation manages production and distribution of product; calibrating the supply of raw material to the capacity of plant, monitoring output and quality controls and assuring prompt delivery." He ensures that the trains destined for the death camps run on time.

Adolf Eichmann was that individual German mandated by Nazi authorities to arrange the logistics for the extermination of large numbers of Jews as if they were threatening germs or disease-carrying rats. Analogies to germs and rats, or, more broadly, vermin, were commonplace in Nazi parlance. For Thomas Merton, Eichmann is also a universal figure of the modern age, a man behind a desk who signs papers and issues directives without moral consideration of what he is signing or issuing. For Merton, Eichmann lives anywhere in any time. He is as common in Washington and Tel Aviv as he is in Beijing and Berlin.

He thrives where institution and bureaucracy, nation and nationality, power and obedience supersede individual freedom and human need. He gains ascendancy whenever charts and numbers trump human feelings, and abstract theories are considered more important than individual lives. As Merton himself says, speaking in the voice of Eichmann in *Conjectures of a Guilty Bystander*, "Your world is full of me, I am all over the place, *I am legion.*" The social philosopher Hannah Arendt, in her study of Eichmann in *Eichmann in Jerusalem: A Report on the Banality of Evil*, stresses his banality. The Trappist monk Thomas Merton, in his studies of Eichmann, in poetry and prose, stresses his universality.

Merton simultaneously sees Eichmann as a specific mass-murderer—an individual responsible for the planning of the destruction of millions—and as a representative figure of his time, and ours. He is the efficient problem solver and the sycophantic servant of the state known for his "blind obedience," even "corpselike obedience." The strength of Thomas Merton's response to Eichmann lies in Merton's seeing him as more than a well-groomed, well-tailored Nazi who reads Hebrew and speaks a little Yiddish. For Merton, Eichmann embodies the technological mindset, where life's complexities are problems to be solved and mechanical efficiency is the highest form of morality.

When given the task of solving "the Jewish problem," Eichmann supports Zionism and encourages large-scale Jewish emigration to Palestine. He soon realizes that too few members of European Jewry are interested in going. Likewise, he fails in his plans of evacuating Jews to Madagascar, and in his proposal for the establishment of a Jewish territory in the Nisko region of Poland. He then turns to a more efficient method of ridding Europe of Jews: mass murder by gas. Eichmann is a rational man without feeling or compassion and without guilt or anxiety. He is the Tin Man, the man without a heart. He is a variation on Swift's narrator in "A Modest Proposal," the sort of person who puts efficiency and profit ahead of children.

Thomas Merton directly addresses the question of Adolf Eichmann on three occasions. He writes an essay on Adolf Eichmann in 1964 called "A Devout Meditation in Memory of Adolf Eichmann," which is published in *Raids on the Unspeakable*. The essay subsequently appears in William H. Shannon's gathering of Merton's social essays, *Passion for Peace*. He makes notes, on pages 286 to 290, on Eichmann in his journal *Conjectures of a Guilty Bystander* in 1965. In his "Epitaph for a Public Servant," he doesn't so much write about Eichmann as he inhabits him for ironic and satiric purposes. He chillingly replicates Eichmann's voice and world view. In a fourth work, "Chant to be Used in Processions Around a Site with Furnaces," Merton recreates the Eichmann personality type but acknowledges Rudolf Hess, rather than Eichmann, as being the source for his satire. Both works are Swiftian performance pieces, as is made clear in Michael W. Higgins's *Heretic Blood*.

"Epitaph" is originally written for *Ramparts* in 1967 and posthumously included in *The Collected Poems*. "Chant" is first published in the *Catholic Worker* and Lawrence Ferlinghetti's *Journal for the Protection of All Beings* in 1961. It is subsequently reprinted in *Emblems of a Season of Fury* and *The Collected Poems*.

In the construction of his chant in 1961, which he sometimes refers to as "the Auschwitz poem," Merton applies his reading of William L. Shirer's *The Rise and Fall of the Third Reich* to artistic purpose. As Michael Mott documents in his biography of Merton, included in Shirer's book are letters "from German manufacturers of lethal gas and crematorium equipment to the camp authorities." Merton takes information from the letters to construct an extended found-poem.

Merton's narrator speaks in the Nazi manner of thought and language. In content, the prose poem links to Merton's *Devout Meditation*. In style, it bears closer resemblance to "Original Child Bomb," about the dropping of the atomic bomb on Hiroshima and Nagasaki, another of Merton's Swiftian performance pieces. *Chant*, written largely as an unpunctuated rant and verbal projectile, clips along at a furious pace.

How we made them sleep and purified them

How we perfectly cleaned up the people and worked a big heater

I was the commander I made improvements and installed a guaranteed system taking account of human weakness I purified and I remained decent

How I commanded

The title of the prose poem "Chant to be Used in Processions around a Site with Furnances" combines monastic words ("chant," "procession") with more clinical terms, such as the passive voice "to be used," the abstract noun "Site" and the comparatively modern term "furnaces." Throughout the Swiftian satire, filled with the unconscious irony of a speaker who has no idea that the very words he boasts of ("I commanded," "I improved") condemn him, Merton has the speaker hang himself by his own diction.

The speaker of the monologue mixes old words with new words and simple words with technical words. The verb "installed" and the nouns "guaranteed" and "system" sit near the ludicrously moronic phrasing of "a big heater." The speaker reveals himself to be at once vacuous and technically sophisticated. He sounds like an American astronaut with his mixture of baby talk and technical jargon. He has no images in his prose, no metaphors, no emotion; his is the prose of statement and euphemism, the prose of clinical and detached discourse.

Whatever the problem, the speaker surmounts it. Whatever the demands of cost, he finds cheaper ways to effect mass destruction. He makes soap from gassed bodies.

> How I commanded and made soap 12 lbs fat 10 quarts water 8 oz to a lb of caustic soda but it was hard to find any fat

He transports corpses, which he euphemistically refers to as "customers," cheaply.

> "For transporting the customers we suggest using light carts on wheels a drawing is submitted"

He knows precise numbers.

> "I am a big commander operating on a cylinder I elevate the purified materials boil for 2 to 3 hours and then cool"

He conducts the right tests.

> For putting them into a test fragrance I suggested an express elevator operated by the latest cylinder it was guaranteed

The speaker dramatizes the Nazi penchant for euphemism. As Hannah Arendt points out, words such as "killing" or "extermination" are never used in Nazi correspondence or directives. The word for murder is replaced by the phrase "to grant a mercy death"; gas rooms are disguised as showers and bathrooms; the gassing centres at Aushwitz and other death camps are called "Charitable Foundations for Institutional Care." In his essay "Auschwitz: A Family Camp," Merton notes that "Officialese has a talent for discussing reality while denying it …." Central to the officialese of Auschwitz is "a pathological joy in death."

Merton asserts that "All of it is the celebration of boredom, of routine, of deadness, of organized futility."

Officialese predates and postdates Eichmann or any other Nazi official. In one of his last essays, "War and the Crisis of Language," written in 1968, Merton points to the "pompous and sinister jargon of the war mandarins in government offices and military think-tanks" where "a whole community of intellectuals, scholars … spend their time playing out 'scenarios' and considering 'acceptable levels' in megadeaths." According to Merton, "Their language and their thought are as esoteric, as self-enclosed, as tautologous as the advertisment … they are scientifically antiseptic, business-like, uncontaminated with sentimental concern for life—other than their own. It is the same basic narcissism, but in a masculine, that is managerial, mode." Nazi officials for Merton enflesh masculine narcissism in the managerial mode.

In language as powerful as Orwell's in "Politics and the English Language," Merton in "War and the Crisis of Language" speaks of "the illness of political language." Political language is "characterized everywhere by the same sort of double-talk, tautology, ambiguous cliché, self-righteous and doctrinaire pomposity, and pseudoscientific jargon that mask a total callousness and moral insensitivity, indeed a basic contempt for man." Eichmann's language, and the language of his associates, is the managerial norm in imperial political systems. Such language is, for example, the voice of officialdom in the United States from Erlichman and Haldeman in the Nixon White House to Cheney and Rumsfeld in the Bush White House.

In 1963, Merton reads Hannah Arendt's *New Yorker* magazine coverage of the Eichmann trial. Arendt's series of articles are subsequently published as *Eichmann in Jerusalem: A Report on the Banality of Evil*. Arendt concludes that "The trouble with Eichmann was precisely that so many were like him, and that the many were neither perverted nor sadistic, that they were, and still are, terribly and terrifyingly normal."

In a July 24, 1963, letter to the Jewish scholar Gershom Scholem, Arendt moves away from an earlier position on Eichmann as an embodiment of "radical evil" and asserts her new position that Eichmann's evil "possesses neither depth nor any demonic dimension" and is best characterized by the adjective *banal*. Only the good, she argues, has depth and can be radical.

Inspired by his close reading of Arendt in *The New Yorker*, Merton writes his "A Devout Meditation in Memory of Adolf Eichmann" in 1964. The title is of course meant ironically, in the way that Swift's "A Modest Proposal" is meant ironically. Merton's meditation is no more devout than Swift's proposal is modest.

"One of the most disturbing facts," Merton notes, echoing Arendt, "that came out in the Eichmann trial was that a psychiatrist examined him and pronounced him *perfectly sane*." In fact, according to Hannah Arendt, "half a dozen psychiatrists had certified him as 'normal'." Far from being some inhuman monster, Eichmann appears all too human. Merton implies that had Eichmann been pronounced insane, his organizational assistance in the destruction of six million Jews would have been easier to fathom.

Merton's analysis of Eichmann in his "Devout Meditation" connects in sentiment, though not in form, to Leonard Cohen's 1964 "All There Is To Know About Adolf Eichmann" in *Flowers to Hitler*. In his synopsis of Eichmann's physical features, Cohen stresses his normalcy: medium eyes, hair, weight and height, even medium intelligence. He has no distinguishing features. In fact, he has ten fingers and ten toes, just like most human beings.

Like Cohen, Merton emphasizes Eichmann's normalcy. He also investigates his troubling sanity:

> We equate sanity with a sense of justice, with humaneness, with prudence, with the capacity to love and understand other people. We are relying on the sane people of the world to preserve it from barbarism, madness, destruction. And now it begins to dawn on us that it is precisely the *sane* ones who are the most dangerous.

In his "devout" meditation, Merton moves from the particular to the general, from the individual Eichmann to the universal Eichmann:

> It is the sane ones, the well-adapted ones, who can without qualms and without nausea aim the missiles and press the buttons that will initiate the great festival of destruction that they, *the sane ones*, have prepared ... No one suspects the sane, and the sane ones will have *perfectly good reasons*, logical, well-adapted reasons, for firing the shot. They will be obeying sane orders that have come sanely down the chain of command ....

Merton questions the value of sanity disconnected from love. He asks what sanity means when it "excludes love, considers it irrelevant, and destroys our capacity to love other human beings, to respond to their needs and their suffering, to recognize them also as persons, to apprehend their pain as one's own."

He concludes his essay by acknowledging Eichmann as not just one person in history but as a recurrent character-type in history:

> No, Eichmann was sane. The generals and fighters on both sides, in World War II, the ones who carried out the total destruction of entire cities, these were the sane ones. The ones who have invented and developed atomic bombs, thermonuclear bombs, missiles, who have planned the strategy of the next war, who have evaluated the various possibilities of using bacterial and chemical agents: these are not the crazy people, they are the *sane* people ...

Merton's final sentence, in a paradox worthy of Swift or Orwell, reads: "... in a society like ours the worst insanity is to be totally without anxiety, totally 'sane'."

In 1967, Merton returns to Eichmann, this time using Swift and Arendt to maximum effect. He deploys the Swiftian technique of becoming the other, of taking on the voice and manner of the enemy for the purpose of mockery and subversion. As Edward Said says in his essay "Swift as Intellectual," Swift's technique "is to become the thing he attacks, which is normally not a message or a political doctrine but a style or a manner of discourse." The speaker in Merton's "Epitaph for a Public Servant," *In memoriam—Adolf Eichmann*, parodies Eichmann's speech patterns.

The dramatic monologue, or word collage, has interesting points of convergence with Denise Levertov's

"During the Eichmann Trial," published in *Jacob's Ladder*. Both Levertov and Merton extensively borrow Eichmann's words from Arendt's reporting in cobbling mosaics of self-deception and blind obedience. Levertov reaches a similar conclusion to Merton's: Eichmann is us. As she so ably puts it, "he, you, I, which shall I say?/... an apparition/telling us something he/does not know: we are members/one of another." Poets—Cohen, Levertov and Merton—add to our knowledge of a mass murderer. Merton's "Epitaph," in my estimation, is his most brilliant and successful subversion of Eichmann's language and personality.

As in his earlier "Devout Meditation," Merton emphasizes Eichmann's sanity in his "Epitaph." The speaker, the voice of Eichmann, tells the reader that his relations with his father, mother, brother and sister are "most normal/ Most desirable." His Christian education is "Without rancor/Without any reason/For hating." He follows orders; he subordinates himself to "The Leader." He, being a grown-up, thinks "Repentance is/For little children." He is, after all, "A man with positive/Ideas/ With no ill will/ Toward any Jew."

Merton in his "Epigraph" has Eichmann say, "Official orders/Were my only language." The words echo Arendt's quotation from Eichmann that "Officialese is my only language." Arendt adds that "the longer one listened to him, the more obvious it became that this inability to speak was closely connected with an inability to think, namely, to think from the standpoint of somebody else." He was also "a non-reader except for newspapers." His banality consisted of "empty talk" and "stock phrases"; he was "genuinely incapable of uttering a single sentence that was not a cliché"; he was, in short, not stupid but vacuous.

Hannah Arendt speaks of Eichmann in the past tense. Thomas Merton speaks of him in the present tense. For Merton, Eichmann lives. He is legion. He is found in every corner of the technological world. Every day, new Eichmanns sign papers, issue directives and conduct desk murder. When an administration, as in the United States, increases its defence budget by billions and reduces its medicare budget by millions, the direct consequence is that poor people who happen to be sick die. As Merton prophetically scolds, "Do not think yourself better because you burn up friends and enemies with long-range missiles without ever seeing what you have done." Similarly, do not think yourself better because you sign a paper in an air-conditioned room without ever witnessing the dying face of a sick person who lacks the money to pay for an expensive operation.

By ovens, or missiles, or neglect, there are many ways to murder human beings while sitting at a desk, and there are many Eichmanns in all parts of the world who are willing by their signatures to commit the murders.

VII

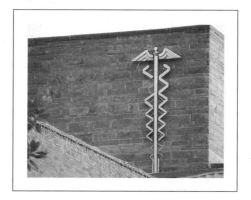

Lover

She came out looking lovely and joyous in a light dress, long hair flying in the wind, face literally shining with love. From that moment (11:45) until I left her (about 4:10) it was simply perfect. We talked and loved and scarcely ate anything, but drank Chianti and read poems and loved ...
    —"A Midsummer Diary," in *Learning to Love*

I am going to write maybe a new book now, in a new way, in a new language too. What have I to do with all that has died, all that belonged to a false life? What I remember most is me and M. hugging each other close for hours in long kisses and saying,
    "Thank God this is at least real."—*Learning to Love*

S pring tingles. Summer burns. It sizzles, it sings. Now
and then, a life-altering summer comes along, one
that leaves you in a different state than it found
you. Maybe it's the summer of '42 or the summer of '08.
It knocks you down and spins you around. You lose the
anchorage of habitual selfhood and surrender to irrational
and contradictory impulses. You fall in love. You fall, and
keep falling. English has the right verb to go with love.

For Thomas Merton, the summer of love and falling
is the summer of '66. He's lying in a hospital bed, vulnerable and dependent, and a young student nurse half his
age walks into his room to bathe his wounds. It's March;
he's reading Albert Camus. One conversation leads to
another, one visit leads to another, and by midsummer,
Merton celebrates his nurse as if he has known her a long
time: "M. is terribly inflammable, and beautiful, and is no
nun, and so tragically full of passion and so wide open," he
writes in his *Midsummer Diary*, the 23,000-word diary he
writes in a week.

When M—she frequently remains an initial in Merton
scholarship to protect her privacy—enters Thomas
Merton's life, she breaks through his defences and over-
turns his habits and patterns. She is the watershed event
in his emotional life. Their physical and psychological at-
traction doesn't lead to sex, but it does lead to a remaking
of the self. After M, there are no more abstract, disembodied sermons on love, no more theoretical speculations
elevating spirit over flesh. Merton begins to see love in the
concrete, in the real, in wholeness. Love intensifies life; it
completes it. He can truthfully say long after he and M go
their separate ways,

Love is our true destiny. We do not find the meaning of life by ourselves alone—we find it with another. We do not discover the secret of our lives merely by study and calculation in our own isolated meditation. The meaning of our life is a secret that has to be revealed to us in love, by the one we love.

By the end of 1966, Merton is prepared to say lines that Oprah can quote in bold print in the February '06 issue of her magazine: "The question of love is one that cannot be evaded ... from the moment you are alive you are bound to be concerned with love, because love is not just something that happens to you: It is a certain special way of being alive." Merton is a poet, a literary and social critic, and a monk. He is also a lover, a man who loves many things in the world, and in one glorious summer, loves one particular person in the world.

Before M, Merton's relationships with women are deeply unsatisfying. "I suppose I regret most my lack of love, my selfishness and glibness (covering a deep shyness and need of love) with girls who, after all, did love me ... My great fault was my inability really to believe it ...." He describes sex as "something I did not use maturely and well, something I gave up without having come to terms with it." In his Cambridge years, he is known as a womanizer and party man. He impregnates a woman. For this and other unbecoming behaviours, he is asked to leave Clare College.

M is the reincarnation of his earlier dream-women, Proverb and the Chinese Princess. She is "flesh, blood, presence, and charm," in Michael Higgins's phrase. Strangely, long before his encounter with his Louisville nurse, Merton dreams of the feminine receiving him and blessing him. His drawings, a large number of which portray the female face, also prefigure such an encounter. Merton doesn't need dreams or drawings to tell him what he most lacks: the touch of a woman. He subtitles his summer diary "Or the account of how I once again became untouchable."

A simplistic definition of a monk is someone who obeys an abbot. A more negative definition is someone who lives without a woman's touch. All that is to change in the summer of '66 when, like an overheated schoolboy, Merton surreptitiously meets, phones and writes his girlfriend against the strictures of his Order. Before M, Merton has friendships with women: with Sister Mary Luke Tobin, his editor Naomi Burton Stone, and his Gethsemani neighbour Tommie O'Callaghan, who shares picnics with him and names one of her sons after him. He loves these women, but he is not in love with them.

Throughout his life, revelations, like dreams, visit Merton in abundance: in the churches in Rome to which his father takes him as a boy, in an old Cuban church where he is on holiday before entering the monastery, on Fourth and Walnut in Louisville where everyone shines love, and before the Buddha statues in Polonnaruwa on his final journey. He is prone to life-altering experiences and, afterwards, to high-blown rhetoric about the experiences. On the church in Havana: "that Heaven was right in front of me, struck me like a thunderbolt and went through me like a flash of lightning." In Polonnaruwa: "I have now seen and have pierced through the surface and have got beyond the shadow and the disguise."

Arguably, no revelation shakes him as profoundly as the revelation that he can give love to a woman and receive it from her. His relationships with women in the past, by his own self-criticism, tend to be more about receiving than giving. They represent a long chain of failed reciprocity. They lack the balance he reaches with M. One thinks of a line in a Nat King Cole song: "The greatest thing you'll ever know is just to love and be loved in return." The line is recycled in the film *Moulin Rouge*, where the painter-dwarf Toulouse-Lautrec screams it from the ceiling of a theatre.

In an earlier chapter, I've pointed to transformations or decisive turnings in Merton's life. He turns to serious reading in 1937, and reads his way to faith. He turns to serious political analysis in 1961, and writes his way into significant political thought. In the summer of '66, he turns again. This time to love. If a monk can be enraptured by spiritual reading and political philosophy, why can't he also become enraptured by a beautiful and loving woman?

In a 1958 letter to Boris Pasternak, Merton first reveals the girl of his dreams, who later incarnates in the flesh of M.

> One night I dreamt I was sitting with a very young Jewish girl of fourteen or fifteen, and that she suddenly manifested a very deep and pure affection for me and embraced me so that I was moved to the depths of my soul. I learned that her name was "Proverb."

The dream occurs in February. A few days later, while on an editorial errand to Louisville, alone on a crowded street, Merton sees that everyone is Proverb, that in everyone there shines her beauty and purity and shyness, even though people don't know who they are and feel ashamed of their names.

He catches another glimpse of the young Semitic woman in an artwork by Victor Hammer. Proverb continues to tag along in the merger of his dream life and waking life. On July 2, 1960, while in St. Anthony's hospital in Louisville, he has a Proverb-like dream in which he is awakened by the "soft voice of the nurse" …. Later on, he thinks he sees Proverb in the flesh, "a Jewish girl sitting on top of the filing cabinets with her shoes off," in a Cincinnati museum. Out of these dreams and visitations, he writes his most beautiful prose poem, "Hagia Sophia."

In late November of 1964, Proverb again comes to him in a dream, this time in the form of a Chinese princess. She comes to spend the day with him. He feels "overwhelmingly the freshness, the youth, the wonder, the truth of her, her complete reality, more real than any other, yet unobtainable." Who says monks live boring lives?

Merton remembers the Proverb-like Ann Winser, a thirteen-year-old whom he had seen briefly in his midteens. He describes her as "a dark and secret child" in "the quiet rectory." "She was the quietest thing in it." He remembers that he had forgotten about her, but also that she had made "a deep impression" on him. To Merton, she represents "the part of the garden I never went to …." She was the "true (quiet) woman with whom I never really came to terms in the world, and because of this, there remains an incompleteness in me that cannot be remedied."

On March 23, 1966, while in hospital for spinal surgery, Merton meets a student nurse who has a fiancé in Vietnam. She has grey eyes and long black hair and bears a strong resemblance to the Proverb of his dreams. Her name is M (S in the Mott biography), and he falls head over heels in love with her. He is almost thirty years her elder.

Spring turns to summer, and in the summer of '66 for the first time Merton falls in love with a real flesh-and-blood woman. No longer theory or theorem, love is incarnated in personhood. We know so little about her, this nurse-dynamo, this mystery girl who topples and re-constructs a monk. Merton burned her letters. We have his journal entries and diary but not her responses. We have one-way communication, him without her. We have fifty pages of a summer diary, perhaps the most courageously honest and self-critical, the most existentially hopeful and despairing of his career. Did he ever put more of his topsy-turvy emotions into a single piece of writing—all his confusion, ambivalence and contradictions?

Occasionally, M makes an appearance in the diary in the lines Merton quotes from her: "The happiest I have ever been is when I took care of you in the hospital ... Being without you isn't the hardest thing—it's not being able to give you anything except thoughts and prayers ... You keep me, you guard me, you protect me in all my ways ...." She tells him that she is so totally his that he'd never be able to get rid of her if he tried. In a sense, they don't let go of each other. Merton continues to write to her until his death in Bangkok.

Merton gives love and receives it. He and M talk about *The Sign of Jonas*, the *Peanuts* comic strip, and *Mad* maga-zine. He writes poems to her. When they get to know each other intimately by letter, phone call and visit, they share their enthusiasm for Joan Baez's "Silver Dagger" by playing it exactly at 1:30 a.m., when M finishes her shift and Merton rises an hour earlier than usual in the hermitage. In the song, the lover tells the beloved not to sing love songs because the mother is "sleeping here/Right by my side." The mother is armed with a silver dagger in her right hand. She refuses to give her permission for union. The song ends with the line "I sleep alone in my bed." The song re-enacts the story of M and Merton.

Did the mother in his mind or the mother in his monastery prevent his marriage? Did the mother-image or the mother-church paralyze his will to act?

In *A Midsummer Diary For M*, Merton tries to explain, rationalize and justify his ambivalent behaviour. He wants M and doesn't want her, he trusts her and doesn't trust her, he's going to leave the monastery and he's not going to leave the monastery. He acts like Hamlet and stutters like a character in Beckett. He must go on with his vocation; he can't go on, he will go on, he won't, he will, it's impossible. He wants to gamble on love but he can't throw the dice. He speaks of "the tyranny of diagnosis." He recognizes that "Lucidity does not prevent anguish."

By the end of the summer, Merton arrives at the view that he has a gift and an obligation to offer his gift to the public. His gift is his living out "an inner dimension of experience" that is desired by many but is closed to them. It is not closed to him. "I know I have to read, and understand, and think, and grasp, and experience," he writes. "I have a rich life, but built on the central cost of cruel deprivation ... But I know that I am not in a position to choose another kind of richness: that of love and living with M." He thinks that he will find his way, in his usual fashion, "without a map." What is important to him is that, perhaps for the first time in his life, he has been fully accepted, understood and loved by another human being.

Such clarity and resolution do not, however, prevent the dark nights of the soul. "What will I be without her? What will she be without me?" he cries in anguish on June 23, 1966. And then directly to M he says, " I do not know how on earth I am going to live without ever seeing you again, talking to you, being with you, loving you warmly and directly, pressing you to myself and kissing you. It will have to be, but I do not know how it is going to be, or how I am going to stand it ...."

Alone in his bed, he dreams dreams of failure and blockage:

He sees her in an unrecognizable lake. She looks disconsolate. He goes down to the lake dressed in his habit and waves to indicate that he is coming. She looks disbelieving. He wants to join her even if it means swimming naked. There appears to be no one around, but as he moves towards her, he finds a monk sitting on the bank obstructing his way. He cannot get to her. He wakes up in great distress.

He phones M to tell her that he is going to meet her. He is seeing her often again. He is going to meet her. He can't find the way.

He finds himself in a place with Buddhist nuns. A printed partition separates him from them. He hears their soft erotic laughter as they become aware of him. He feels himself drawn to them.

The monastery building (Gethsemani) is on fire. The fire burns slowly in the inside of the building. It threatens to spread. There are people still in the building. He thinks to himself, "Why don't they get out?" He is in the burning building but moves through small patches of fire to safety. The building is not destroyed but most of what is inside is consumed.

He's on a voyage. He's with a dark girl. The two of them decide to wear kilts. He thinks that he will put on the MacGregor Tartan to identify with his ancestors. But the red colour is startling, unfamiliar. Images flash into consciousness: islands, journey, bull, horse. The dark girl releases the bull, but they are safe.

In the heat of his love affair, he dreams of his mother, in his mind the cerebral woman whom he loses when he is six and whom he frequently associates with coldness and sternness. Unlike the "black mother" of his dreams, who dances with him, his real mother judges him. He dreams of a "tangle of dark briars and light roses." His attention singles out one beautiful pink rose. The rose becomes luminous. He becomes aware of "the silky texture of the petals." At this point, his Mother's face (he capitalizes the word Mother) appears behind the roses. The roses vanish.

Has his mother come back to chastise him? In the dream, she seems to disapprove of his rose.

Novelist Tom Robbins, in *Still Life with Woodpecker*, posits that there is only one serious question in life: "Who knows how to make love stay?" Merton has love in his hands and lets it go. He experiences "the greatest thing," knows how to make it stay, and deduces that if he gives himself to love completely, he will end up destroying himself and M.

In cool-minded hindsight, which may be as appropriate for the post–love affair as overheatedness is during the affair, Merton concludes that the way of the family man is not to be his way in the world. He has chosen the way of the monk, a "rich life" built on "cruel deprivation."

Even for a many-sided man like Merton who is happier to be many things than one thing, he cannot be both a monk and a lover, a husband and a monk. Sometimes either/or is the only choice. Merton gives up love and sacrifices the touch and lifelong blessing of a woman in order to live out fully his commitment to silence and solitude (the traditional way of being a Trappist) and his commitment to public discourse in his essays and poems (the non-traditional way of being a Trappist). The Order tolerates his letters to the world, but not his being "a priest with a woman."

For one glorious summer, Thomas Merton lives out John Howard Griffin's insight that to be moderate in matters of love is simply not to love. He also takes to heart the advice of his psychiatrist friend Dr. Jim Wygal to be careful not to destroy himself. No fire burns more brightly than the fire of love, and no fire consumes as completely. In perhaps his most searing lines in the eighteen poems Merton writes to and about M, these unforgettably stand out: "If only you and I/Were possible." His words bring the fire into language, and the brevity of his expression makes the anguish all the more devastating.

What Merton learns from his summer conflagration is beautifully expressed by Albert Camus, whom Merton is reading in the summer of '66. "When you have once seen the glow of happiness on the face of a beloved person, you know that a man can have no other vocation than to awaken that light on the faces surrounding him …." For his remaining two summers, Merton lives out these lines.

VIII

Always a Synthesizer

I write, therefore, I am.—*Journals*, VI

Thomas Merton develops an inventory of the self before Oprah and Dr. Phil, before self-talk and narcissistic talk shows become trendy. Almost every work in his canon is a new Book of Self; each of his nearly four thousand letters and each poem in his thousand pages of poetry has to do with some new exploration of the self, some new metaphor of selfhood. His Cartesian formula in the early years is not only "I write, therefore, I am," but also "I write about the self, therefore, I must have one."

John Berger, in *Keeping a Rendezvous*, reminds us that autobiography "begins with a sense of being alone. It is an orphan form." It is Thomas Merton's most frequently used literary form, whether in narrative prose or journal. Even his poetry reflects the emotional and spiritual condition of his mind and heart at a given moment in time. The orphan chooses an orphan form. In a 1939 journal entry he writes, "Anything I create is only a symbol for some completely interior preoccupation of my own."

Merton realizes that the talent of the novelist, of being able to make imaginary beings real, does not belong to him. He performs best when he is writing about himself and the things he loves, real things and real people. He communicates best when he constructs mirrors, or metaphors, of his interior longing and dreams. His talent lies in his ability to generate new metaphors of the self to match his ever-changing personhood, to peel back petal after petal of disguise and delusion, of conformity and convention, until he reaches a self without the need of masks, a self that can trust the mercy and love and mystery of its surroundings.

The Catholic philosopher Charles Taylor, in *Sources of the Self*, makes the point that the self develops "in relation to certain interlocutors." The self exists within what he calls "webs of interlocution." Merton's interlocutors are missing. To compensate for the lack of early and significant interlocutors—later in life he certainly doesn't lack correspondent-interlocutors—he carries on a lifelong conversation with himself about himself. He continuously tells and retells his own inner story, for he has a strong need to hear it. He has few significant others to whom to tell his story, and the early memories he does have are charged with ambivalence: the memory of a critical mother and the memory of a father more interested at times in his art and his girlfriend than in his son.

Merton is forced to work hard at being the architect of his own identity; he creates the images of self that are not reflected to him by his family, images that would otherwise be unaffirmed. No doubt M's affirmation of his worth must have carried enormous weight. She blesses him in a way that no other woman, including his mother, was able to do.

One of the intriguing facts of Merton's life, however, is that he has no sooner achieved his hard-won sense of self than he is willing to abandon it. He no sooner finds himself as a writer when he wants to lose himself as a hermit; he is willing, in a sense, to return to spiritual orphanhood, to "Daily zero," in his own phrase, as a needy man rather than maintaining the self-image of an important writer, a respected monk, and an ebullient bon vivant. But, as Merton often reminded his readers, to lose a self implies having one to lose. The ego-self has to be strong in order to be abandoned. In his final address in Bangkok, Merton advances the idea of having a strong self and then losing it in transformation from "self-centered love into an outgoing, other-centered love." Does one hear M's voice behind this proclamation?

You would expect Thomas Merton to construct interesting metaphors for the self simply because he had so much practice. But there are other reasons for his striking metaphor generation. He has two-eyed vision: the vision of a monk and the vision of a poet, the monk's meditative seriousness and the poet's ease with words. Who but a monk and a poet could define himself as neither a white-collared man nor a blue-collared man nor a Roman-collared man, but rather a "Man without a Collar"? He also reads voraciously.

Vast reading deepens and broadens his sense of self. Merton is, after all, one of the great readers of the century, someone akin to Carl Jung in his subject range, from existentialism to psychoanalysis to Sufism, from poetry to Buddhism to theology. He reads widely in every field except the natural sciences. Author and critic Guy Davenport colourfully spells out Merton's uniqueness as a writer and reader: "When he wrote about the Shakers, he was a Shaker. He read with perfect empathy: he was Rilke for hours, Camus, Faulkner ... I wonder whether there has ever been as protean an imagination as Thomas Merton's."

The number of works read, quoted and commented on, for example, in *The Asian Journal* alone is simply staggering. In the thousands of volumes he read in his lifetime, it would not be an exaggeration to say that he would have read hundreds that in some way or other commented on the self. At Columbia, where he encountered another poet-priest, Gerard Manley Hopkins, about whom he planned to pursue a doctorate, he doubtless would have come upon these words: "A self then will consist of a centre and a surrounding area or circumference, of a point of reference and a belonging field ...." Merton's point of reference is his monastery of Gethsemani; his belonging field consists of correspondents across the globe.

Among many works read on the self and selfhood, pivotal works such as D.T. Suzuki's Zen essays and the Sufi psychotherapist A. Reza Arasteh's *Final Integration in the Adult Personality* stand out. According to David D. Cooper, Arasteh gives Merton "a new reading of his personal history" or, more precisely, a new way to read his personal history. Important works on spirituality about Indians of the Americas reviewed in his *Ishi Means Man* additionally play their part in his growth. In native America, Merton discovers "a conception of identity which is quite different from our subjective and psychological one, centered on the empirical ego regarded as distinct and separate from the rest of reality." In American Indian thought, "one's identity was the intersection of cords where one 'belonged'"; one is simply a branch on a tree with its roots in the ancestors and guardian spirits and its trunk connected to the family and tribe. The self, as Hopkins implies, is always surrounded by something larger than itself.

T.R.V. Murti's *The Central Philosophy of Buddhism*, read on Merton's Asian journey, proves to be a rich catalyst for his final thoughts on the self. Merton frequently copies quotations into his notebooks, such as "To accept a permanent substantial self is for Buddhism the root of all attachment," though he is also quick to record that "the Madhyamika does not deny the real; he only denies doctrines about the real. For him, the real as transcendent to thought can be reached only by the denial of the determinations which systems of philosophy ascribe to it." In the Buddhist dialectic, the person presumably may be a part of what is real, but what we understand to be the self, a permanent fixed identity, is an illusion. In the same way that there is no abiding "milkness," in Buddha's own analogy, since milk can become curds or cheese or ice cream, so there is no abiding self other than self-concepts that attempt to freeze it.

Merton's readings, then, freshly define and explore the self. Arasteh's book, for example, which Merton reviews in detail in "Final Integration: 'Toward a Monastic Therapy'," inspires him to write one of his most comprehensive summing-up statements of the transcultural self in general and his own transcultural self in particular: "He has a unified vision and experience of one truth shining out in all its various manifestations ... He does not set these partial views up in opposition to each other, but unifies them in a dialectic or an insight of complementarity ...." Arasteh gives Merton the confidence that he can pass through the tunnel of neurosis, despair and personal crisis and come out the other side stronger, healthier and more·integrated. His afflictions can be spurs, not inhibitors, to growth.

M's contribution is also of enormous significance. M, through her love, demonstrates to Merton that he is lovable, someone worth loving.

Merton's metaphors of the self remain remarkably consistent throughout his life. Seeds. Fire. Desert. Mercy. Mountains. Mountains figure prominently in his work from beginning to end, a fact his official biographer, Michael Mott, is quick to take advantage of in calling his biography *The Seven Mountains of Thomas Merton.* Merton writes about mountains, and if one grants mountain status to knolls, he lives near them for most of his life.

Ron Dart in *Thomas Merton and the Beats of the North Cascades* catalogues the peaks, inner and outer, that Merton ascends and descends throughout his life: "Canigou, The Calvaire, Brooke Hill, The Pasture, Merton's Heart, Mount Purgatory, Mount Olivet and Kachenjunga." You can't step into Merton without stepping into "his literary and spiritual appreciation of mountains and peaks as waymarks and cairns for the spiritual and contemplative journey."

In that haunting first sentence of *The Seven Storey Mountain*—"On the last day of January 1915, under the sign of the Water Bearer, in a year of a great war, and down in the shadow of some French mountains on the borders of Spain, I came into the world"—he begins to sketch his first famous metaphor of the self in pilgrimage. The metaphor suggests an ongoing climb to new stations of awareness and realization. In the Western tradition, the mountain embodies one of the principal metaphors of verticality and hierarchy, presupposing a base, a summit and, frequently, a climber.

The mountain in Merton's context is an aggressive metaphor; the mountain is something to be scaled and overcome; each storey is to be left behind for a higher and better one until one reaches the top, which for Merton at the time is to be a monk in the Cistercian Order. *The Seven Storey Mountain* is an aggressive book. Not only does Merton's young soul reach for new heights of spirituality, but he is willing to abandon those on lesser slopes—Protestants, Marxists, hedonists and non-believers.

Twenty years later, in his Asian journey, Merton has dramatically shifted metaphors. He is no longer the questing pilgrim, the aggressive climber; he is the marginal man, for the monk is "a marginal person who withdraws deliberately to the margin of society with a view to deepening fundamental human experience." He replaces a vertical metaphor with a horizontal one. His new metaphor of the self is not concerned with up or down, high or low, but with the concept of the circle. Far from conceiving himself as one triumphantly atop a mountain, Merton now sees himself as someone at the margins, occupying the furthest point from the centre of the circle. As he acknowledges in an earlier work, "Philosophy of Solitude," the "deep 'I' of the spirit, of solitude and love, cannot be 'had,' possessed, developed, perfected. It can only be ...." Notably, large portions of *The Asian Journal* concern the mandala, where no one soul has a higher status than another.

When Merton engages the mountain metaphorically at all in *The Asian Journal*, it is with the mountain disentangled from a conquering verticality. His mountain now is "the side that has never been photographed and turned into post cards"; the mountain with "another side," not susceptible to climbing or photography. The many-sidedness of the mountain captures his attention, but he again chooses to identify himself with the "margins"—the side of the mountain that is not seen, that cannot be seen.

In *The Asian Journal*, Merton follows his brief meditation on the mountain with a meditation on doors, the three doors that are one door: "the door of emptiness," which "cannot be entered by a self"; "the door without sign," which is "without information"; and "the door without wish," which "does not respond to a key." These doors are "without a number" and have "no threshold, no step, no advance, no recession, no entry, no nonentry."

As with the metaphor of the mountain, Merton starts with the familiar (a door) and proceeds to deconstruct the metaphor until it is strange and foreign; he denudes the metaphor of its usual connections and connotations. The door, which usually symbolizes a passageway to a new stage or beginning, in Merton's context is freed from transformative successions and is simply something there.

Merton, who so effortlessly slips from Buddhist metaphors—the mountain that is no-mountain, the door that is no-door—to Christian metaphors, closes the meditation with the thought that Christ is the "nailed door" (the crucifixion) and the no-door (the resurrection), which is "the door of light, the Light itself."

Merton's door, like his new mountain, is not something to be dominated or controlled or even sought. "When sought it fades. Recedes. Diminishes. Is nothing." The door "cannot be entered by a self" or opened by a key. Merton has come a long way from aggressive Western metaphors of the self to more "passive" Eastern metaphors in which the ego-self or false self must be abandoned in order for the true self to emerge.

Note that Merton is frequently concerned with truth and falsehood in his metaphoric usage: the true mountain of silence and the false mountain of tourism, the true door without label and the false door of labels. The metaphors of the true and false selves, which he seems to have appropriated from Saint Bernard, have a long history in his writing, and are another of his consistent metaphors.

Merton points out that in both the biblical and Buddhist traditions, freedom from the ego-self is a necessary stage in human growth. Biblically, Merton informs novice monks in his lecture "The True and False Self," true freedom consists of "freedom from idolatry," acknowledging that sometimes "the real idol is me." Merton further emphasizes, in another of his lifelong metaphors, "If I want my idols to go into the fire, I myself must go into the fire." While the Bible associates sin with self-idolatry, Buddhism also encourages detachment from the illusory self, the self as object. Both traditions compel adherents to shed the "everyday conception of ourselves as potential subjects for special and unique experiences or as candidates for realization, attainment and fulfillment."

What happens to Merton in the intervening years between his first major autobiographical work and his last autobiographical notebook is a deepening experience of "selfhood" and a deepening understanding of Zen as a technique to lift the false veils covering one's true face. Zen, as he says repeatedly, is not a doctrine, a body of knowledge, or a religion but a means whereby one might see and awaken. Zen's great metaphors have to do with vision and wakefulness.

Even those awake and seeing may miss important things. Merton notes that D.T. Suzuki, from whom he learned a great deal, sometimes falls into the kind of dualistic thinking he criticizes others for falling into: "... his lineup of Buddha vs. Christ is also dualistic, and when he starts that he forgets his Zen .... It seems to me the Cross says just as much about Zen, or just as little, as the serene

face of the Buddha." More lightheartedly, in a letter to
Suzuki, Merton links himself and the Gospels to Zen:

> I have my own walk and for some reason or other Zen is right
> in the middle of it … with all its beautiful purposelessness
> … it has become very familiar to me though I do not know
> what it is … I'll say simply that it seems to me that Zen is
> the very atmosphere of the Gospels, and the Gospels are
> bursting with it.

To see, in a Zen context, implies that one is blind, and
to awaken implies that one is asleep. Zen seeks to awaken
the somnolent person and to liberate him from the prison
of his own ego. The master shocks or disorients the novice
by a koan or a kind of theatre of the absurd—hence the
crack of bamboo on one's head or the spilling of tea in one's
lap to unlock the prison.

As early as *The Seven Storey Mountain*, Merton recognizes himself as a "prisoner of my own violence and my
own selfishness." Throughout his writings, and by means
of his writings, he seeks "the awakening of the unknown 'I'
that is beyond observation and reflection and is incapable
of commenting upon itself." This "Zen" way of looking at
the self is perhaps best expressed in the journals of the
early sixties, published in 1965 as *Conjectures of a Guilty
Bystander*:

> The taste for Zen in the West is in part a healthy reaction
> of people exasperated with the heritage of four centuries of
> Cartesianism: the reification of concepts, idolization of the
> reflexive consciousness, flight from being into verbalism,
> mathematics, and rationalization. Descartes made a fetish out
> of the mirror in which the self finds itself. Zen shatters it.

The metaphors at work in Merton's psyche in the last years of his life are often drawn from Zen or Zen-like sources. The sixties foment his consciousness, but not so much from new seeds—another favourite Merton metaphor—but from the harvesting of old seeds planted in his Columbia University years. In the late 1930s, for example, his friendship with the Hindu monk Bramachari, his reading of A.K. Coomaraswamy, and his exposure to Aldous Huxley's *Ends and Means* have already propelled him towards Eastern philosophies.

In his 1939 Columbia University Master's thesis on William Blake, he prophetically quotes Chuang Tzu, the Chinese sage whose poems he will later refashion into English, and in his notes for the thesis he makes reference to D.T. Suzuki, an authority on Zen with whom he will later spend "rap" sessions in New York City. In a letter to Aldous Huxley, November 27, 1958, Merton pointedly writes, "May I add that I am interested in yoga and above all in Zen, which I find to be the finest example of a technique leading to the highest natural perfection of man's contemplative liberty." His sixties metaphors of the self, then, are not really new constructs, but new articulations of old metaphors.

In his 1963 *Emblems of a Season of Fury*, in poems such as "The Fall," "Song for Nobody" and "Love Winter When the Plant Says Nothing," and in "Night-Flowering Cactus," one begins to see the influence of Zen reshaping his ways of seeing and understanding the self. In "The Fall," for example, he writes,

> There is no where in you a paradise that is no place
>   and there

You do not enter except without a story.
To enter there is to become unnameable.
Whoever is there is homeless for he has no door and
    no identity with which to go out and to come in.

The poem, in part, seems to prefigure what Merton will say in his meditation on doors in *The Asian Journal*. There, Merton makes the point that no one "with a self can enter," and here, five years earlier, he asserts "he who has an address is lost."

In *The Way of Chuang Tzu* (1965) Merton continues with what I have chosen to call Zen metaphors, though one might as correctly say Taoist metaphors. In "The Man of Tao" he writes,

No-Self
Is True-Self
And the greatest man
Is Nobody.

In another poem in the same work, "The Empty Boat," Merton, through the mask of Chuang Tzu, says that the "perfect" man goes through life "like Life itself/With no name and no home ... His boat is empty." Subsequent prose works—*Mystics and Zen Masters* (1967) and *Zen and The Birds of Appetite* (1968), a work of joint meditation with D.T. Suzuki—push forward the insight that the "true self" is the "no-self."

In a kind of Zen lexicon, visible in his poetry and in his Asian works, Merton speaks of the self as "nobody" found "nowhere" in "nothing." The meaning of these words eclipses their presence: they are and are not; they self-destruct. The self, for late Merton, is without name and address, even without attribute. The self is indistinguishable from what is around it, indistinguishable from the Christian Godhead, Heidegger's Being, Chuang Tzu's Tao, Buddhism's Mind, Hinduism's Atman or Sufi's Self. Interestingly, in Merton's epiphanies from Louisville to Polonnaruwa, he envisions oneness, not separation. He collapses boundaries and embraces the essential oneness of the self and the other.

The picture of the self Merton finally draws is without name and address, but it is neither alienated nor isolated; rather, the self throws itself at Mercy and propels itself towards Love. As Merton himself puts it in *The Asian Journal*, "Our real journey in life is interior: it is a matter of growth, deepening, and of an ever greater surrender to the creative action of love and grace in our hearts." Again, one hears echoes of M's impact in his words.

Merton's journey takes him back to the "orphaned," "no thing" self. He uses the paradoxes of Christianity and Zen to break free from linguistic imprisonment and to burst the cultural bubbles that shield us from the realization of our nakedness, aloneness and utter dependency on the mystery outside ourselves. He comes to point zero fairly naturally from long practice in geographic and psychic displacement. He is a man without a country whose home is a monastery; he is without a family, property or social status. He is a marginal man who aligns himself with those on the margins.

As Merton phrases it in his last notebook, "The self is merely a locus in which the dance of the universe is aware of itself as complete from beginning to end—and returning to the void. Gladly. Praising, giving thanks, with all beings. Christ light—spirit—grace—gift …."

IX

Journal Keeper

And I have always wanted to write about everything. That does not mean to write a book that covers everything—which would be impossible. But a book in which everything can go. A book with a little of everything that creates itself out of everything. That has its own life. A faithful book. I no longer look at it as a "book."—*Journals III*

On what turns out to be his last trip, a trip to Bangkok to deliver a talk on Marxism and monasticism, Thomas Merton travels with a small book of Anaïs Nin short stories called *Under the Glass Bell*. He copies one particular sentence into his notebook from the story "The All-Seeing." He notes that the mariner "never attaches himself to what he sees." His "very glance is roving, floating, sailing ...." He has "a sense of the distance one can put between oneself and one's desires, the sense of the enormousness of the world and of the tides and currents that carry us onward." Merton's recording of Nin's sentence provides an apt summary of his journal-keeping vision and techniques in *The Asian Journal*, the on-the-spot record of his last days.

Parisian-born Anaïs Nin writes the longest, most continuous journal of what it is be a woman in the twentieth century. The journal is her confidante, her refuge, her birth canal. Prades-born Thomas Merton writes one of the longest, most continuous journals of what it is to be a man in the twentieth century. The journal is his second self, a source of reflection and pause for a fast-moving life. Nin keeps a journal for over sixty years, Merton for over forty. Hers begins as love letters to call a wayward father home; his, initiated by his mother and called *Tom's Book*, begins as a way to keep New Zealand relatives up to date on his shenanigans.

The personal journal or diary is, in novelist Joyce Carol Oates's estimation, the most seductive of art forms. Who isn't attracted to writers' interior lives, their dirty linen or closeted skeletons, their everyday gossip and banter? The last journal of a writer is particularly seductive. In

Merton's case, *The Asian Journal* contains his last prayer, poem, speech, photographs, encounters, his last dreams, his last notes on the world. The journal is the art form in which Merton achieves his fullest disclosure of self, his holiest transparency.

Nin's journals, handwritten in brown and purple ink, comprise 35,000 pages, and by her own estimate, 200 volumes. Merton keeps spiral notebooks for readings and bound notebooks for his own thoughts. He affirms his identity by keeping a close watch on his mental, physical and emotional experiences. She starts writing her journals at age eleven and continues into her seventies. Her father's abandonment precipitates immigration to the United States. She is unsuccessful in her attempts to restore her broken family. Merton's journals begin when he is about thirteen and continue until his death at age fifty-three. They are, in part, perhaps, a compensation for the loss of motherly attention.

In *Tom's Book*, his mother notes that at age two he has a vocabulary in both French and English of 160 words; many of the words are bird names. He also, according to her notes, has 16 teeth, is 34 inches tall, and weighs 30 pounds. Later in life, Merton follows his mother's pattern of noting bodily detail, the aches and pains of being alive. Perhaps his narcissism begins with hers.

The final journals of both writers (Merton's in 1968, published posthumously in 1973) and Nin's (covering the period 1966 to 1974, published posthumously in 1980) record the sights and sounds of Asia: Merton on India, Sri Lanka, Singapore and Thailand; Nin on Japan, Cambodia, Singapore, Thailand and Bali. They even stop in some of the same places, stay over in the same hotel and write about the same things.

For example, Nin characterizes Singapore as

Mixed races in the street could have been interesting but they were drowned in noise. Cars, rickshaws and bicycles … the riders insult each other. Dirt. Open sewers. Open shops. Much hawking …

Merton depicts Singapore as "the city of transistors, tape recorders, cameras, perfumes, silk shirts, fine liquors …." It has "a Chinese kind of practicality and reality along with the big Western buildings which, as it happens, are clean and well-kept."

Both journal keepers evoke sensuous details for their descriptions, though they differ on the details. Nin emphasizes the dirt, Merton the cleanliness of the city. More significantly, Merton uses the present tense, which seems more immediate and intimate than Nin's use of the past.

The Oriental Hotel in Bangkok, which once played host to Joseph Conrad and Somerset Maugham, elicits comment from the two more recent sojourners. Nin has this to say about the hotel:

The Oriental is the oldest and most famous hotel. I stay in the old wing where I love the teakwood rooms and the beautiful gardens sloping down to the river … I open my window and see the wide river glittering in the evening light. An Esso sign on the banks outshines the other lights. I had hoped to see Bangkok before its destruction by Western culture ….

And Merton this:

I go to the Oriental, which is thoroughly quiet. The road
from the airport could be a road from any airport—from
Louisville to Gethsemani in summer. The same smell of hot
night and burning garbage, the same Pepsi billboards. But
the shops are grated up with accordion grilles, the stucco
is falling off everything, and the signs in Thai are to me
unintelligible.

In Merton's return stay in the hotel, his residence is
a "fine split level dwelling high over the river" entered
"through an open veranda on the other side, looking out
over the city."

In these entries about the hotel, Nin's use of the
present tense coincides with Merton's, her physical detail
matches or exceeds his, her moral indignation is more
overt, and both remark on the presence of American
capitalism—Esso and Pepsi—in the Thai landscape.

In his book *A Book of One's Own: People and Their
Diaries*, Thomas Mallon lumps Nin and Merton together
as pilgrims. Merton in the early years bounces about
more than Nin: "From Prades to Bermuda to St. Antonin
to Oakham to London to Cambridge to Rome to New
York to Columbia to Corpus Christi to St. Bonaventure
to the Cistercian Abbey of the poor men who labor in
Gethsemani." Both are people who go places, even if the
journey is primarily to ever-deeper parts of the self. Their
final geographical and interior journeys converge, as do
their family histories.

Both lose parents at an early age: Merton's by death,
Nin's by abandonment in the case of her father and es-

trangement in the case of her mother. Both are brought to the United States, and Nin, perhaps even more than Merton, keeps the perspective of an outsider. Both have artistic parents. Merton's father is a painter and his mother has a gift for dance and the arts. Nin's mother is a singer, her father a composer and her brother a pianist. Both have lifelong attachments to artists and the arts. Among Nin's close friends are Henry Miller and Lawrence Durrell, along with Artaud in theatre and Noguchi in sculpture. Merton is close to the painter Ad Reinhardt, the poet Robert Lax, the printer Victor Hammer, and is pen pals with Nobel laureates: the Russian novelist and poet Boris Pasternak and the Polish poet and memoirist Czeslaw Milosz.

Their final journals also share a great deal in common. Merton's Asian journal is a travelogue, a photo album, a reading list—quintessential Merton, as the back cover proclaims—a book of quotations, a manual on Buddhist meditation, even a menu and bar list. Nin's Asian journal is also a travelogue and photo album, in addition to being a book of letters (received and sent), a reading list and a dream diary. Their final journals are such grab bags that one is reminded of French theorist Jacques Derrida's words on the postcard: is the stamp central or the address or the picture or the message?

In *The Asian Journal*, does the text consist of travel observations and reflections with a subtext of quoted readings, or is it the reverse? The Merton text is riddled with editorial comment, bibliography, speeches, poems and letters and assembled by several editorial hands. The Nin text is so studded with letters as to resemble an epistolary novel. Both journals seem less a single flowering than a garden in bloom.

The Asian Journal in particular is pre-eminently the sort of book that Walter Benjamin aspired to, consisting more of quotation and reactive thought than of original thought, the sort of book Noam Chomsky likes to write, in which the notes exceed the text, and the sort of book Jonathan Swift wrote in *A Tale of A Tub*. There are as many "endings" to Merton's book as there are beginnings to Swift's. The last journal entry is December 8th, followed by a postscript, sputtering into Part Two, complementary reading, and brought to a slow conclusion with nine appendixes, a bibliography, a glossary, picture credits and an index. The journal proper ends on page 239, yet the book carries on ghost-like to page 445.

Merton aspires to write a book of everything, "a book in which everything can go" and in *The Asian Journal*, thanks in part to his editors, he achieves it. The American photographer Man Ray once said in an interview that the artist sought a confusion or merging of all the arts, as things merge in real life. Merton achieves a similar dream of notes and poems, confessions and meditations all merging into a single wild, but structured and unclassifiable, form. A dabbler in almost every genre and subgenre known to literature, the journal is the form in which Merton seems most at home.

To see connections in life stories and in the contents of their final journals doesn't deny or underestimate their differences. Merton, as much window as mirror, makes more political comment than Nin. He makes clear his opposition to the Vietnam War, his championing of civil rights, his advocacy of peace, his criticism of capitalism. The monk in his cabin in one sense writes to no one but himself, and in another sense, addresses the world at large. Merton's humour is also stronger than Nin's; his observations on nature more frequent.

There is no journal in his vast output that does not respond enthusiastically to the nature around him. His eye is always turned outward as well as inward, as in this entry from *The Asian Journal*: "Two white butterflys alight on separate flowers. They rise, play together briefly, accidentally, in the air, then depart in different directions."

Nin is more self-consciously literary than Merton. She is a theorist as well as a practitioner of the journal as an art form, and in her Asian journal, compared to his, more insistent on taking her inner temperature. Her journals are contrived, laboured over, edited and re-edited. She belongs to the French literary tradition of the journal going back to Montaigne's autobiographical essays in the sixteenth century and running through Rousseau's confessional disclosures in the eighteenth to André Gide's journals and Proust's novels in the twentieth. Her journals are "a way to taste life twice, in the moment and in retrospection."

Nin posits two human needs in relation to creative writing: the need to document one's day-to-day life, the inner journey, and the need to leave something permanent behind: the myth. The first need, Nin argues, is met by journal writing, and the second by fiction, which transforms experience into myth. Her practice, however, contradicts her theory. Her journals more successfully than her fiction transform document into myth; the quotidian is elevated to art and the timebound achieves timelessness. Nin's brother has called her journals the best novels that she ever wrote.

Merton's journals owe something to the seventeenth-century Japanese haiku artist Basho in his fusions of travel and spirituality, and to the New World tradition of journal keeping from the time of Columbus in the fifteenth century. The stranger in a new land records his observations. The outsider makes himself real through words. Merton also draws from the intense literary self-interrogations of Thoreau in the nineteenth century. Additionally, his journals connect with the spiritual tradition of the journal going back to Saint Augustine and running through Pascal's thoughts to Bonhoeffer's letters from prison. Merton's Asian journal partakes of all these traditions: a man dialoguing with his own soul, a stranger observing a new land and a literary man fully at ease in his form.

The journal as an art form engenders some of Thomas Merton's best writing. Merton himself confirms this point of view. In a letter to June J. Yungblut (March 8, 1968), he writes: "The work I feel more happy about is at once more personal, more literary, more contemplative. Books like *Conjectures*, *New Seeds*, *Sign of Jonas*, *Raids* ...." Two of these books—*Conjectures* and *Sign of Jonas*—are journals, and one of the books, *New Seeds*, is journal-like in form. In *The Secular Journal*, Merton remarks that he has grown tired of reading novels and that the journal is what he likes to read and write: "Gallery proofs of *Secular Journal* make it clear to me that my best writing has always been in journals and such things—notebooks."

In his finished journals, Merton refines casual jottings into meditations, in a manner somewhat akin to Pascal's *Thoughts*, whereas the unfinished *Asian Journal* is written in haste, "almost stenographically" in phrases and put into sentences by the editors—a maquette rather than a finished piece of sculpture. And yet, curiously, the words Merton uses to describe *Conjectures* can as accurately be applied to *The Asian Journal*: "… a series of sketches and meditations, some poetic and literary, others historical and even theological, fitted together in a spontaneous, informal, philosophic scheme in such a way that they react upon each other." Robert Lax shrewdly observes, "In his journals Merton came closest in a verbal medium to the spontaneous self-expression that he achieved in his calligraphies."

The Asian Journal, companion and cousin in some ways to his other Asian works—*The Way of Chuang Tzu, Mystics and Zen Masters, Zen and the Birds of Appetite*—may be likened to his Zen drawings, a kind of word jazz in which the quick of life is caught in the quick of writing. By the mid-sixties, Merton comes to the view that he needs to integrate his interests and divergent selves and that the journal form is best suited for the integration. The journal, like an Irish stew, puts anything with everything, poetry with politics and prayer. All his dreams, realized and unrealized, can co-exist in a common space. He no longer imposes artificial boundaries between the spiritual and the artistic or the secular and the sacred.

The Asian Journal, for instance, comprising "Asian Notes," the continuing journal for 1968 ("The Hawk's Dream"), and a small pocket notebook effortlessly braids the spiritual and the secular, travelogue and meditative quotation. Merton records soccer scores and arcane theological points and makes notes on butterflies and Eastern philosophies. The journal, that most democratic of art forms, puts all entries on an equal plane; no one part aristocratically reigns over another part. The form is inherently anti-climactic and serendipitous. What is stumbled upon is commented upon. The miraculous inheres in the mundane, the extraordinary in the commonplace. "It's all real," in Merton's own phrasing. Likewise, for Anaïs Nin, the journal form has no climax, no resolutions of conflict, no denouement, only more entries.

In *The Asian Journal*, Merton records his response to the Buddha statues in Polonnaruwa, but it is not a road to Damascus experience. However deeply he was affected by the serenity of the statues, he carries on with his observations and his journal gives equal attention to a great many things. He complains about his cold and sore throat; he buys too many books; he notes that stocks are up in Hong Kong, there is no complimentary champagne en route to Bangkok, a soldier reads the Bible on his way to Vietnam, Hong Kong beats Singapore in soccer, Paz resigns as Mexican ambassador to India, Jackie Kennedy remarries, Johnson halts the bombing, two magpies fight in a tree, he prefers Ceylonese beer to Indian. Polonnaruwa is simply part of the goulash.

As with Merton, so with Nin. Her last journal begins with her reaction to Japan and ends with her response to Bali. Between these two ports of call she acknowledges a positive reception to her journals, she receives an abundance of fan mail, she battles cancer, she records her dreams, she delivers commencement addresses at colleges, and so on. In her final journal, no one event or thought or feeling or dream dominates another; no epiphany or peak experience subordinates all others; everything reacts upon everything else. In the democracy of the journal, each experience comes with its own space and voice.

One of the charming aspects of Nin's Asian journal, for example, is its attention to food. The journal is a Babette's feast of culinary delights. About Japan, she writes:

> I am eating a variety of vegetables I do not know. I recognize small green pepper, eggplant, watercress and cucumber—and a variation of the sweet potato, parsnip, dandelion, cucumber flower. I eat fried chrysanthemums … Only the Japanese would think of serving red watermelon in a green plate. Or wrap rice in green leaves.

The journal form gives Merton the opportunity to accept his tensions. He goes on his Asian journey with questions for which he hopes he will find answers, and with conflicts he hopes to resolve. On November 18, he chides himself: "Too much movement. Too much looking for something: an answer, a vision, something other. And this breeds illusion, illusion that there is 'something else'." Later he writes, "Now suppose some loon comes up to me and says, 'Have you found the real Asia?' I am at a loss to know what one means by 'the real Asia'. It is all real as far as I can see."

Again, his dreams are telling. His problem of how to get to the next place is dissolved in his forgetting what the problem is; the balloon with the explosive gas which he tries to throw away refuses to go away, but neither does it explode.

Merton's breakthrough in *The Asian Journal* is not so much to change his life as to accept it. Two central books much quoted in *The Asian Journal*—T.R.V. Murti's *The*

Central Philosophy of Buddhism and Giuseppe Tucci's *The Theory and Practice of the Mandala*—encourage him not to escape into idealism but transform consciousness into a detached and compassionate acceptance of the empirical world in its interrelatedness. The Madhyamika attitude, akin to Nin's mariner who doesn't attach himself to what he sees, lives with tensions without resolving them. Merton doesn't need to choose between writing and spirituality. He can pursue both and integrate both.

The journal form for Nin is crucial to her identity. When her roots are severed in the family diaspora, the journal is her only link, if only imaginary, to the father root. When her self-image is buffeted by publishing firms rejecting her novels, the journal restores her confidence. In bold print, Nin screams in *House of Incest*: DOES ANYONE KNOW WHO I AM? It is the cry of journal keepers, of those who symbolically repair their fractured identities by writing.

As early as her first journal, she writes, "Playing so many roles, dutiful daughter, devoted sister, mistress, protector, my father's new-found illusion, Henry's needed all-purpose friend, I had to find one place of truth, one dialogue without falsity." She has to create a world of her own "like a climate, a country, an atmosphere in which I could breathe, reign, and recreate myself when destroyed by living …."

Merton too knows about loss. When his family tree is cut down, he becomes a branch disconnected from his trunk and roots. He, too, abandons one country for another, one language for another, one lifestyle for another. The bohemian becomes a hermit; the poet, a monk. The journal becomes for him a symbolic repair shop, a way of restoring lost things, of reuniting the splinters of a fragmented self.

Paradoxically, by employing the most narcissistic of art forms, both Nin and Merton are able to get out of the self by burrowing deeper into the self: Nin largely through psychoanalysis and Merton largely through Zen. Before one can lose a self, one must find a self to lose. As Michael Mott jests, "The koan for Thomas Merton might have been 'How does one write about self so that the self disappears?' ... 'By exhausting the subject of self'." In *The Sign of Jonas*, Merton's own way of putting it is: "Let me at least disappear into the writing I do."

Merton fears, as Nin does, the prison of self. Her favourite words often begin with the prefix *trans*: "transcend, transmute, transform, transpose, transfigure," words that connote moving beyond the self and across to other selves. The prefix for Merton is surely *re*: restore, remake, revitalize, retrieve, reform, words suggestive of something being lost and reintegrated. As Nin puts it, "the theme of the diary is always the personal, but it does not mean only a personal story: it means a personal relation to all things and people. The personal, if it is deep enough, becomes universal, mythical, symbolic; I never generalize, intellectualize. I see, I hear, I feel." The more Merton and Nin develop a self, the more they give it away; the more they speak personally, the more they reach a universal audience.

In his Calcutta speech, included as a part of *The Asian Journal*, Merton clarifies his sense of self by identifying himself as a monk and, as a monk, a marginal person connected to those relegated to the fringes of society: Afro-Americans, Latin Americans, Native peoples, poets, hippies and the disenfranchised generally. Merton's self is in solidarity with the selves of those who are "irrelevant," a word Merton uses in his talk.

Nin's late correspondence, much of it included in her last journal, bears testimony to the truth of her assertion: "The more I developed my self, the less mine it became." In letter after letter, readers inform her that in writing about herself she wrote about them. Thousands of Merton readers would say the same thing about Merton in his journals. What Nin desired in her early journals, embodied by the Gaelic word *furrawn*, which means "talk that leads to intimacy," both she and Merton accomplish in their final journals. In his "Preface to the Japanese Edition of *The Seven Storey Mountain*," Merton articulates his understanding of *furrawn*.

> Therefore, most honorable reader, it is not as an author that I would speak to you, not as a story-teller, not as a philosopher, not as a friend only; I seek to speak to you, in some way, as your own self …

The self in such intimacy porously opens to the dreams and fears of others.

In their last journals, two talented mariners write their own stories, and in writing theirs, write ours.

X

Hello, Goodbye, Hello Again

[The] living line and the generative association, the new sound, the music, the structure, are somehow grounded, in a renewal of vision and hearing so that he who reads and understands recognizes that here is a new start, a new creation. Here the world gets another chance. Here man, here the reader discovers himself getting another start in life, in hope, in imagination.
—Thomas Merton, "Paradise Bugged," *Critic*, XXV

He walks, says Robert Lax, like a dancer. James Laughlin learns some Sanskrit and something about Eastern religions so he can understand the notes for *The Asian Journal* and then for years afterwards lets words like *dzogchen* and *sunyata* float in his head so he can be near his dead friend. Lax waits for him on the island of Patmos. Jack Kerouac dedicates poems to him. He ping-pongs into Allen Ginsberg's dreams. He is the world's pen pal. And I've been a kind of cheerleader for him, a proselytizer for his work, along with hundreds of other nameless ones who have responded to his photogenic face, his firecracker walk, and his "'Aaahhhh!' to life."

It's not easy saying goodbye to a monk, especially one you've hung around with for the last thirty years. Monks with moon faces, with beautifully flawed and cracked porcelain lives, with warm, human laughs who are sometimes mistaken for Henry Miller or Pablo Picasso are especially hard to let go of. They're stickier than gum, as unshakeable as smoke. My monk looks down impishly upon me in my study, denim jacket over cassock, his hand underlining a script. I write under his smiling face and prayers: "Give me humility in which alone is rest and deliver me from pride which is the heaviest of burdens." And my favourite, "My Lord God, I have no idea where I am going."

Just when you think it's time to let go, to move on— you can't be a cheerleader all your life—something tugs you back. Some unfinished business, you tell yourself. Shouldn't everybody in the world know this monk in the blood the way you do? If only you write one more piece, frame one more window so others can see the monk as you do, lean on his strength as you've done, then you can call it quits. Don't you have a special relationship with this monk? Or isn't that at least the illusion he continues to foist and the delusion you continue to embrace?

There was a time when it seemed that I was making discoveries about the world as he was making them, and they were the same discoveries. I'd be reading Rilke, and then I'd read about him in his journals reading Rilke. I'd come upon Robinson Jeffers in my reading, and a day or so later I'd read about his having stumbled upon Jeffers. And so it went with Czeslaw Milosz, Max Picard and a host of others. It seemed that as I was making up the world he was, too, and I'd go to where he had gone or sometimes get there before I read of his already being there. Does that make any sense?

Closing time doesn't come easily when your life seems to be bleeding into somebody else's or somebody else's life seems to be bleeding into yours. You're having a blood transfusion, and you've built up a dependency. Then, out of the blue, to make matters worse, years after his death in Bangkok, his private journals fall into your lap, and you're tempted to go on: one more conference, one more speech, one more paper, one more essay, one more Thomas Merton weekend at Five Oaks in Paris, Ontario, one more …

What do you take away from an encounter with a monk? Maybe something as simple as this: be who you are, stay in the flesh, stay on the earth, laugh when you can, love as much as you can. Again, Lax clairvoyantly sums up a life in a phrase: *hermit at the heart of things*. My connection to Merton has always been more emotional than intellectual. You could almost say, if saying so made any logical sense, more physical than spiritual.

His face haunts me. It's surprisingly photogenic. His face doesn't wear time; he doesn't age theatrically. He moves a short distance from young and bald to middle-aged and bald, the final face a little chubbier than its earlier versions. It's not that I don't remember his insights into Christianity, or Zen and Sufism for that matter, but ideas are not the wine with which I fill my stomach. Rather: "Tom, the great laugher. God, was he ever that! Open-mouthed 'Oh Ah Ha' with head thrown back, hands on hips." That's what Ron Seitz remembers in his "memory vision" in his *Song for Nobody*, and that's what I'd like to retain in mine.

Merton is a man I've felt along with, thought with, argued with, laughed with, dreamt with. I've been trying to let go. But he's been such a big part of my mental life over the years it's like letting go of part of myself. I've reviewed his letters to writers. I've written a poetic documentary on his life and work. I've compared him to Anaïs Nin and Wendell Berry. I've written a poem about him—imagining him in Las Vegas—surveyed his metaphors and his changing theories of the self, and lectured on his impact on the poet Denise Levertov and the literary critic Frank Lentricchia. But there's still so much more to say.

I'm as dumbfounded by what has fallen away as by what has persisted and deepened. The romance with M holds little interest for me now. The epiphanies, even the one in which he sees through the shadow and the disguise before the Buddha statues at Polonnaruwa, mean less to me now than they once did. It's not that I discount mystical experience—in no way whatsoever would I want to mock any aspect of human experience beyond my ken—but the ordinary grips more tightly now than the extraordinary. To the quotidian I am beholden. I'm also no longer interested in whether he had a son in his Cambridge days, whether the son died or whether he continues to live off the royalties from *The Seven Storey Mountain*. I'm not interested in the degree to which the electrocution was purely accidental or partly due to his own carelessness. By Bangkok, it seems to me, Merton had decided to be carefree, even careless. He would take his chances.

What I am interested in more and more is his friendship with Robert Lax. I'd like to meditate on that friendship. How it was sustained largely through letters for decades, how they spoke in their own private language, how they frolicked with different pseudonyms, and how if you blocked off the names you wouldn't always be sure who was speaking. The voice of one would take on the nuance and timbre of the other, and each would anticipate the other's moods and moves.

As I write these words, I'm aware of James Harford's recent publication entitled *Merton & Friends: A Joint Biography of Thomas Merton, Robert Lax, and Edward Rice*. Harford realizes that no one's story is complete without the intersection of other lives and stories. You can't fully tell Merton's story without telling at the same time Lax's and Rice's. Every human life is an intersection in New York City where avenues from all directions feed into the centre. Merton's life feeds off a thousand other lives-—from the living and the dead, from family (blood relatives and fellow monks), friends, correspondents and strangers. You need all the women from his mother to M to Joan Baez and all the men from William Blake to Jacques

Maritain and Brother Patrick in order to reconstruct his life and thought.

I'd like to go more deeply into Merton's dreams. A dream analysis of *The Asian Journal*, perhaps, where his night mind ferries from dream to dream, from balloons to clothes. I'd like to reread *The Asian Journal* with Edward Said's *On Late Style: Music and Literature Against the Grain* in hand. Merton's last works, including his long, difficult poems, *Cables to the Ace* and *The Geography of Lograire*, like his Zen calligraphies, resist easy interpretation. They're antipoems in the Nicanor Parra vein; they have the stubbornness of a Zukofsky poem. "[W]hat of artistic lateness," Said asks, "not as harmony and resolution, but as intransigence, difficulty and unresolved contradiction?" Said then goes on to quote the social philosopher Theodor Adorno: "The maturity of the late works does not resemble the kind one finds in fruit. They are … not round, but furrowed, even ravaged. Devoid of sweetness, bitter and spiny, they do not surrender themselves to mere delectation."

Have I made Merton too easy, too tidy—too tame? Isn't Merton towards the end furrowed and spiny? Isn't he, in Said's words, "nonharmonious" and full of "nonserene tension"? Yes and no, perhaps.

I'd like to look at his failures, the work that doesn't get done. I'm thinking of the promised writings on Bob Dylan and on art and worship. I'd like to look at the work that doesn't quite work, that doesn't have his patented signature of speaking to someone as if that person were himself. His book on the Bible, for instance, is in some ways a disappointment. It begins with a request from

Rabbi Herschel to generate a book on the Bible for Time-Life. Merton's book makes interesting connections to the Marxist poet and filmmaker Passolini's "The Gospel According to St. Matthew," it connects to psychoanalyst Erich Fromm and Protestant theologians Karl Barth and Dietrich Bonhoeffer, but for all the freshness of vision and novelty of connection, it doesn't get personal. Merton doesn't underpin his reading of the Bible with personal anecdotes and convictions. The voice doesn't seem to be deeply rooted in his body.

How different is Merton's book on the Bible from the one he inspired and encouraged Father Ernesto Cardenal to write: *The Gospel in Art by the Peasants of Solentiname*. (Cardenal helped to found a Christian commune on the islands of Solentiname in Lake Nicaragua.) The book consists of references to scriptural passages and extended commentary by himself, farmers and local artists. It moves beautifully from the Word to words to painted pictures of Christ brought into the everyday lives of struggling and politicized ordinary Nicaraguans. With Merton's artistic talent, his gift for words, his solidarity with the poor and the disenfranchised, one can only regret that he dashes off his response to the Bible too hastily. One can imagine something as wonderful as Cardenal's book.

I'd like to compare Merton to Jack Kerouac, two good old Catholic boys who went a little "Zeny." In his free-falling, tumbleweed prose, Merton can sound like Kerouac, and Kerouac in his meditations on the world can sound like Merton. Here's Merton, sounding like Beat Jack, in a letter to Lax on the death of the black monk of abstract expressionism, Ad Reinhardt:

Make Mass beautiful silence like big black picture speaking requiem. Tears in the shadow of hermit hatch requiems blue black tone. Sorrows for Ad in the oblation quiet peace request rest. Tomorrow is solemns in the hermit hatch for old lutheran reinhardt commie paintblack ... Tomorrow is the eternal solemns and the barefoots and the ashes and the masses, oldstyle liturgy masses without the colonels ... Just old black quiet requiems in hermit hatch with decent sorrows good by college chum.

And here's Kerouac in *Desolation Angels* sounding like Zen Tom:

Hold together, Jack, pass through everything, and everything is one dream, one appearance, one flash, one sad eye, one crystal lucid mystery, one word—Hold still, man, regain your love of life and go down from this mountain and simply **be**—**be**—be the infinite fertilities of the one mind of infinity, make no comments, complaints, criticism, appraisals, avowals, sayings, shooting stars of thought, just **flow, flow**, be you what it is, it is only what it always is—Hope is a word like a snow-drift—This is the Great Knowing, this is the Awakening, this is Voidness—So shut up, live, travel, adventure, bless and don't be sorry ....

Different words. The same idiom. The same rhythm.

Merton (often) and Kerouac (almost always) have that informal Yankee drawl that takes you back to Huck rafting on the river, where Hemingway says all good American literature gurgles up from. I'd like to call my imaginary piece "Tom & Jack" and imagine the reaction from staid publishers and stodgy editors. But somebody else can do it. I'm formally done with compañero Merton now. It's time to move on.

Somebody else can do a good psychoanalytical biography, from the British School of Object Relations, and a good Freudian biography, and a good feminist one. Somebody else can analyze his dreams. Somebody else can catalogue his reading. There are plenty of workers in the vineyards. Let them pick the grapes and bottle the wine. I'm happy as a footnote to a footnote in Merton studies, a disposable entry in the bibliography. I once happened to stumble upon the fact that much of Merton's Asian trip was duplicated, unknowingly, ten years later by Anaïs Nin. Call it a small discovery. Enough for me.

Mind you, when I give a paper at the Fourth General Meeting of The International Thomas Merton Society at St. Bonaventure University, I feel the old pull of lingering longer. For the first time I see his handwritten lecture notes from when he was an English teacher at Bonaventure. The experience transports me back to the First General Meeting in Louisville in 1988. There I hear Merton's taped voice in Bangkok, and see his televised face for the first time, hear those final words about standing on your own two feet when the institutions around you are crumbling, feel a power I didn't expect to feel from a guy who sometimes seems confused and ambivalent in the journals.

At Bonaventure, a gorgeous campus with red-tiled Spanish roofs and enough trees and space for walkabouts, I see for the first time Merton's disciplined hand on Pope and the Augustans, on Donne and the Metaphysicals, on Milton, on Shakespeare, dozens of hardcover notebooks. Organized, systematic, insightful, detailed: the notes make my own makeshift lecture notes, written for the most part on throwaway scraps of paper, seem grossly inadequate.

I think to myself how his hand has changed over the years. The hand of *The Asian Journal*, Merton's final notebook, a hen-scratch, indecipherable at times, so rapidly did it try to catch the quick of things. Can a hand reveal a life? In the early monk years following Bonaventure, Merton, in hand and in personality, is tight; he is linear, moralistic, serious, sure of himself. As he goes on, he gets looser, more tolerant, funnier, less sure of himself.

I shouldn't have been surprised at how tidy his Bonaventure hand was. After all, Merton is a consummate man of the arts. You can't think of many in our century more thoroughly artistic. He likes to call his visual work "abstractions" or "graffiti." For him they are "simple signs and ciphers of energy" because "one who makes such nondescript marks as these is conscious of a special vocation to be inconsequent." He takes photographs, he draws, he does calligraphy, he writes novels, he writes poems, he translates other people's poems. Is there an art form in which he does not, at some time or other, dabble and often excel?

I'm particularly fond of the photographs and the Zen drawings, which he sometimes calls bloodstains. Aren't his words bloodstains too? I'd like to connect the final drawings to the final poems and his wide-open spirituality in the last two years of his life. The ink gestures on paper, movements, shapes, signs—call them what you will—come to the viewer without introduction, explanation or justification. They are without name or label. They are, in the same way that the universe is. They declare the mystery and power of the creative presence.

In their mixture of heavy and light, dark and light, chance and control, conscious and unconscious, object and space, lines present and vanishing, his visual bloodstains are born and die in an instant, in a breath, in a single movement of the wrist. Partly given, partly made, they burst forth and self-eclipse; they sing hallelujah and hosanna; they self-pronounce their own alpha and omega. These late visual works don't talk about silence; they achieve silence; they perform it; they come from it and return to it.

Sometimes Merton makes prints of these concretized intuitions, these one-breath markings, by blotting a brush-work image on paper. The blotted image looks different from the mother image, more aerated and porous, more faint, with vanishing detail. In some of the prints what is there is hardly there at all. The invisible seems to have as strong a presence on the paper as the visible.

In my predilection to praise, I find myself wanting to boast about his Zen rooster ink drawing. I want to crow about his photographs of windows and doors and chairs, of simple human objects, and his photographs of walls and rocks and roots and birds, the sleeping Buddhas at Polonnaruwa, the Tibetan child, the standing and arms-folded Georgia O'Keeffe. The will to proselytize itches from time to time. The wholeness, the holy transparency, the superabundance, the surplus, the openness, the recklessness, the wildness, the Zorba-like vitality continue to amaze me.

Robert Lax, the long-limbed, long-faced poet and friend (physically a male Modigliani and a natural mystic), looks at the full artistic production, written and visual, and says: "the poems help the calligraphies, the calligraphies help the poems; the poems and the calligraphies help the manifestoes; you will see; you will see." How right he is. The work is all cut from the same stone, and a deep-seeing friend sees the hidden wholeness to it all. Merton towards the end of his life, it seems to me, is personally aware of the hidden wholeness surrounding everything he does.

Merton readers have their favourite Merton. One of my favourites is *The Asian Journal*, the journal equivalent of his calligraphies and final poems. One breath. One movement of the wrist. His final unedited say about himself and the world. Photo album. Travelogue. Booklist. Buddhist commentary. Letters, speeches, dreams. All quintessentially Merton: his loves, beefs, doubts, passions, speculations, dreams. All very human. No entry privileged over another. The times he drinks too much, the times he has an irritating cold, the times he feels himself levitating in joy are all recorded with equal faithfulness. Here Merton moves on paper the way he moved in life: fast. And he moves in this last journal with a special poignancy. You know it's the end, and you know the truth of John Berger's phrase: "And our faces, my heart, brief as photos."

So what am I going to miss? Certainly not the conferences, though I met good friends there. I've grown tired of my own voice, sick of my own bleating, and less sure that academic minutiae on his life and work will resurrect much of his vitality. The intimacy, I'll miss. The feeling that I had found my writer and wouldn't have to search for another. The feeling that my journey was somehow like his: to burrow down deep into the central stone of the self after scraping off as many false attachments as I could. And in that digging and burrowing and scraping I wouldn't feel alone. I would sometimes hear a voice, a voice I could almost convince myself was his: don't worry, things are okay, there are things you don't know about, and won't and can't, the world does not depend on you, don't carry burdens that aren't yours, mercy is the secret word of the universe, someone will catch you if you fall.

Merton speaks to you as if he were you or you were he or you and he were one. He speaks brother to brother, brother to sister. He cracks open the bi-polarity of the father tongue and mother tongue with a third possibility: the brother-sister tongue. He doesn't lecture from the pulpit or banter from the kitchen but talks from the table at which the two of you are seated. He shows you his cuts and bruises in words as simple as bread, as full-bodied as wine. And when he finishes talking you ask yourself: is he talking about himself or is he talking about me?

You know he has read more because in a monastery you have time to do those things, but inside, in the tormented heart and the stuttering soul, he's just like you and me. That's the illusion Merton persuades you of, at any rate. Here again is how he puts it in his famous Preface to the Japanese Edition of *The Seven Storey Mountain*: "It is not as an author I would speak to you, not as a story-teller, not as a philosopher, not as a friend only: I seek to speak to you, in some way, as your own self ... Who can tell what this may mean? I myself do not know."

The reader, the hearer—for Merton is someone you hear more than read—is witness to a life, privy to the unveiling of a human personality in its struggle to be fully human. The miracle in his writing, in his tone, is that in unveiling his own face he unveils ours; in writing the Book of I, he manages to write the Book of Us.

Merton's ideas are lived, tested, reformulated, retested, relived. They're brought into his bloodstream. What he passes on to you, you know he's lived through, the best of his work existential and experiential. He speaks not "in the language of speculation" but "in terms of personal experience." This, he says, is "always a little hazardous, because it means leaving the sure, plain path of an accepted terminology and traveling in the byways of poetry and intuition … to talk about my own soul." There are very few purely intellectual ideas in Merton that are not first made real by the heart and played out in the sinews of the body.

When you ingest as much as Merton did, you lose the baby fat of cocksureness. You learn to live with your hives of desire, your gourdful of tension. You become at times a little confused, impatient and grumpy (listen to some of his short-fuse lectures to the Novices at Gethsemani), self-obsessed and self-forgetful. You become a little paradoxical but aware of the paradoxes:

> I have also had to accept the fact that my life is almost totally paradoxical. I have become convinced that the very contradictions in my life are in some ways signs of God's mercy to me, if only because someone so complicated and prone to confusion and self-defeat could hardly survive for long without special mercy.

Merton knows himself to be difficult, giving people at times an impression of agitation and rambunctiousness. He finds it difficult to live the spiritual life with the spiritual equipment of an artist. He would have been trying for any superior, one breath going up, another coming down, one shoulder leaning West, the other East. When you read the biographies, you come away with a certain sympathy for Dom James, Gethsemani's head honcho and Merton's sparring partner throughout the fifties and early sixties. Merton can be as wearying as a puppy, even in the journals, when you sometimes want to scream at his insatiable hungers and relentless energies: give yourself peace, man, take a break, have a rest, sleep on it.

I once had the experience of sitting with Merton's friend and secretary and general editor of the personal journals. During a long-winded lecture at the Third General Meeting in Colorado Springs, Brother Patrick Hart fidgeted, yawned, crossed his legs one way and then the other, closed his eyes, opened them and surveyed the room, rested his head in his hands, and so on. I thought to myself: this is what it would have been like sitting beside Merton. A dynamo. The man who walked fast, read fast, typed fast, ate fast, the man with a dozen projects cooking in his head and a dozen books on the go.

I like the fact that Merton never really found a conventional literary form, a genre he could make his own. He's a failed novelist, at times a poet manqué and an uneven essayist. What he does best resides within marginal forms like notes, meditations, journal entries, letters. He's a master of marginal forms, and it stuns me that after two decades of dabbling in story and poem I've only begun to realize that whatever writing talent I may possess has more to do with these marginalia than with the central forms. I, too, am a writer of notes and meditations. I, too, write best about the things I love.

Merton should have taught me the value of the marginal earlier, but I couldn't see the obvious until a poet-friend pointed it out to me. Now, this late in the game, Merton has harvested a new form for me: a controlled chaos, a wild domesticity. The marginal monk wrote notes and that's what I have aspired to and done a little of in my notes on Emily Dickinson, Muriel Rukeyser and Dennis Lee. I would even seek to set down my notes, as he does in *The Sign of Jonas*, in the context "of ambivalence, of questioning, of supreme spiritual risk."

Some writers find their forms, others spend their whole lives searching. Yeats, for example, wrote prophecy, plays and autobiography, but he is remembered for his poetry. And that's what you think of writers. She's a novelist. He's a poet. That one's a playwright. But I like the unclassifiable ones, the ones like Lawrence and Camus and Merton, who try their hand at a variety of forms but never really find the one they're totally at peace with. These ones you take whole, with their flaws and cracks, or you don't take them at all. Me, I want the whole Lawrence—sermons, paintings, diatribes, novels, stories, poems, plays, letters, propaganda, rants—and I want the whole Merton from his *Catch of Anti-Letters* to his final anti-poems. The only thing in the Merton canon I have little patience for is the hack and hagiographic work he did early on for the Church and the monastery: Catholic kitsch and apologetics. On that I'll pass.

There's another cable of connection, more existential, more psychological. I feel marginal most of the time. I feel hyphenated, the way Merton perhaps felt. Not a poet-monk but a poet-teacher, or someone, on the poet side, with delusions of that kind of hybrid grandeur. Like Merton, born on the border of France and Spain, I've always felt border-born, border-crossed, a bit Irish, a bit Canadian, but neither, really. At home nowhere and comfortable only with strangers or foreign things. I understand Merton's fascination with the East, with Buddhism, with multicultural pen pals, psychically, from the inside. It's what I would do given half his talent. Neither this nor that, but something else, but I'm not sure what the something else is. Did he ever feel at home? Have I ever felt at home? When I wrote in *The Thomas Merton Poems*

I am polyglot
not sure which language is native
which country is home
and all my skins are itchy

was I talking as Merton or as myself?

So how do I say goodbye to my moon-monk? There are so many more talks that I want to give.

I want to speak on Merton's concept of the natural, a revered and father-rooted word. I want to think more on his lines about contemplation as "the highest expression of man's intellectual and spiritual life." How contemplation "is spiritual wonder, ... spontaneous awe at the sacredness of life, of being" and "gratitude for life, for awareness, and for being." How "It is a vivid realization of the fact that life and being in us proceed from an invisible, transcendent, and infinitely abundant Source. Contemplation is, above all, awareness of the reality of that Source."

I want to examine Merton's diagnosis of American militarism. "I fear the ignorance and power of the United

States ... The body of a great, dead, candied child. Yet not dead: full of immense, uncontrolled power," he writes. "If somebody doesn't understand the United States pretty soon—and communicate some of that understanding to the United States—the results will be terrible. It is no accident that the United States endowed the world with the Bomb." He goes on in his 1961 journal to pinpoint his diagnosis: "The mixture of immaturity, size, apparent indulgence and depravity, with occasional spasms of guilt, power, self-hate, pugnacity, lapsing into wildness and then apathy ...." I can't think of a more searing and accurate analysis of American imperial power in contemporary thought.

Hello. Goodbye. Hello again. I've been enmeshed in the dialectic of farewell for some time now. Homecoming. Departure. Coming home again. It's time to let go. Time to say goodbye for good.

I want to remember Merton through the words of his student Matthew Kelty: "I would always think of him not as being brilliant and an intellectual and all that, I think of him as being poor, and simple, and little and fragile and dearly loved." I want to remember him through the words of Robert Lax: "he grew to be/the person/he knew/he was." And I want to pass on some last advice. Walk towards him slyly, friend. Slowly. Peek slantedly at his calligraphies, his photographs and prayers, his poems, meditations and notes: those unguarded moments when his heart opens to receive you, and you don't worry where one self begins and another ends.

Chapter Notes

Preface (Merton & Nouwen)

I never met Thomas Merton, but I did have a fleeting encounter with Henri Nouwen. Years ago, an Anglican priest asked if I'd be interested in visiting L'Arche Daybreak in Toronto and if I'd like to meet Henri Nouwen. I said yes. I went along. But I knew nothing about Nouwen. I had read nothing. He was a stranger to me.

At the time, I didn't have the advantage of having read Michael W. Higgins and Douglas R. Letson's words about him in *Power and Peril: The Catholic Church at the Crossroads* (Toronto: Harper Collins, 2003): "Nouwen understood, both as a psychologist and as a spiritual director, that an essentialist spirituality of the manuals, a spirituality disembodied or disincarnate, could no longer speak to people." Looking back, I think I went to Daybreak because I vaguely knew that it was something like Jean Vanier's L'Arche, his home for people with developmental disabilities in France.

The first thing that struck me was how free the people living in the house were with their bodies and emotions. As soon as I entered, I was hugged. Words came later. People laughed and smiled. The body as a whole rather than a single part—the tongue—seemed to be their vehicle of communication. After a half-hour or so of hugs and smiles and laughter, a thin man blew in like a gust of wind. He hugged everyone and was hugged by everyone. He quickly blew out again. I was to read later that Nouwen had experienced a touch-deprived childhood. One can imagine what his new family of touchers and feelers meant to him.

There was silence for a few minutes, and then tongues began to wag about Henri this and Henri that. I then realized that I had met Henri Nouwen. Later that day, Henri blew in again to say a prayer at the ecumenical worship service, and blew out again.

I didn't realize it at the time, but Nouwen was a gift. Years went by. I never thought about him, never picked up any of his books. I've only just begun to read him now. He is quickly becoming as spiritually necessary for me as Thomas Merton. Both invite me into prayer, liturgy and sacrament in radically simple ways.

"the theology of encounter." Merton refers to the theology of "encounter" on July 9, 1965, *Journals V* in the context of his understanding of "The Acts of the Apostles."

"chomp chomp chomp …" comes from the Kentuckian poet Ron Seitz's memory of Merton speaking, in *Song for Nobody: A Memory Vision of Thomas Merton* (Liguori, MO: Triumph Books, 1993).

Dan Berrigan's somersault remark is used as a blurb on the back cover of *The Collected Poems of Thomas Merton* (New York: New Directions, 1977).

I take Henri Nouwen's remarks on meeting Thomas Merton from his Foreword to Esther de Waal's *A Seven Day Journey with Thomas Merton* (Ann Arbor, MI: Servant Publications, 1992).

Robert Waldron, in his *Walking with Thomas Merton* (New York: Paulist Press, 2002), quotes an important Merton passage from *Conjectures of a Guilty Bystander* that reinforces my point on the social gospel: "In a word, if we really understood the meaning of Christianity in social life we would see it as part of the redemptive work of Christ, liberating man from misery, squalor, subhuman living conditions, economic or political slavery, ignorance, alienation."

Richard Holloway, the former Bishop of Edinburgh, further reminds us in his fine little book *Looking in the Distance: The Human Search for Meaning* that "Jesus belonged to that tiny group of men and women in history who instinctively ally themselves with the victims of power." Merton belonged to that tiny group as well.

"Christ of the burnt men" is a phrase Merton uses as his last words in English in *The Seven Storey Mountain.*

A final point of connection between Merton and Nouwen rests in their love of art. Nouwen taught a course at Yale on the spirituality of Van Gogh's paintings and used Rembrandt's painting of the prodigal son as the basis of his most famous meditation. Merton attended Columbia University with the abstract expressionist Ad Reinhardt, owned a Reinhardt painting, and carried on an interesting correspondence with him. He also befriended the printmaker Victor Hammer, and appreciated the paintings of Paul Klee.

Merton has no prolonged gaze at a painting comparable to Nouwen's gaze at the Rembrandt, but he does make an extended comment on one of Reinhardt's "black on black" cross paintings. In *A Search for Solitude,* III, he writes: "Reinhardt finally sent his 'small' painting. Almost invisible cross on a black background. As though immersed in darkness and trying to emerge from it. Seen in relation to my other object the picture is meaningless—a black square 'without purpose'—You have to look hard to see the cross. One must turn away from everything else and concentrate on the picture as though peering through a window into the night. The picture demands this—or is meaningless for I presume that someone might be unmoved by any such demand. I should say a very 'holy' picture—helps prayer—an 'image' without features to accustom the mind at once to the night of prayer—and to help one set aside trivial and useless images that wander into prayer and spoil it."

The above is one of Merton's most detailed and extensive comments on a specific work of art. According to James Harford, *Merton & Friends: A Joint Biography of Thomas Merton, Robert Lax and Edward Rice* (New York: Continuum, 2006), the small black painting is presently housed in a storage vault at Gethsemani, and is worth over a million dollars.

Chapter I (Beginner)

All references to Merton's books are fully recorded in Works Cited, but I do want to draw particular attention to ten or so works that underpin my book:

1. The Journal Keeper: *The Asian Journal*. New York: New Directions, 1973.

2. The Intellectual: *Conjectures of a Guilty Bystander*. Garden City, NY: Doubleday, 1966.

3. The Contemplative: *New Seeds of Contemplation*. Norfolk, CT: New Directions, 1962.

4. The Artist: *Raids on the Unspeakable*. New York: New Directions, 1966.

   Merton is both an artist of the word and the image in this book. For a greater bounty of images, the reader will also want to own Roger Lipsey's *Angelic Mistakes: The Art of Thomas Merton*. Foreword by Paul M. Pearson. (Boston: New Seeds, 2006). If he still has money in his pocket, then *Geography of Holiness: The Photography of Thomas Merton*, edited by Deba Prasad Patnaik (New York: The Pilgrim Press, 1980), is worth purchasing. And if the reader, or should I say viewer, has any money left and is as interested in photographs of Merton as by Merton, then *Father Louie: Photographs of Thomas Merton* by Ralph Eugene Meatyard with an essay by Guy Davenport and edited by Barry Magid (New York: Timken Publishers, 1991) completes Merton's visual library in book form.

5. The Lover: *Love and Living*. eds. Naomi Burton Stone and Brother Patrick Hart. New York: Farrar, Straus, Giroux, 1979;

and *Learning to Love: Exploring Solitude and Freedom: Journals of Thomas Merton*, vol. 6, 1966–1967, edited by Christine M. Bochen. San Francisco: HarperSanFrancisco, 1997.

6. The Poet & Translator: *New Selected Poems of Thomas Merton*, edited with an introduction and notes by Lynn R. Szabo. New York: New Directions, 2005; and *Emblems of a Season of Fury*. New York: New Directions, 1963.

7. The Letter Writer: *The Courage for Truth: The Letters of Thomas Merton to Writers*, ed. Christine M. Bochen. New York: Farrar, Straus and Giroux, 1993.

8. The Social and Political Activist: *Passion for Peace: The Social Essays of Thomas Merton*, ed. William H. Shannon. New York: Crossroad, 1995.

9. The Tone Meister: *The Intimate Merton: His Life from His Journals*, eds. Patrick Hart, O.C.S.O. and Jonathan Montaldo. San Francisco: HarperSanFrancisco, 1999.

10. The Environmentalist: *When the Trees Say Nothing: [Thomas Merton's] Writings on Nature*, ed. Kathleen Deignan, Notre Dame, IN: Sorin Books, 2003.

Zorbamonk. My friend Dan Pilling takes his idea of the dancing monk from the main character in the Greek novelist Nikos Kazanzakis's *Zorba the Greek*.

Of Merton's friends mentioned in this chapter—Lax, Rice, Forest—the only one still living is Forest. I use his Merton biography, *Living with Wisdom: A Life of Thomas Merton* (Maryknoll, NY: Orbis Books, 1991), and Edward Rice's *The Man in the Sycamore Tree: The Good Times and Hard Life of Thomas Merton* (New York: Doubleday, 1970) a great deal in this chapter. William H. Shannon's *Silent Lamp: The Thomas Merton Story* (New York: Crossroad, 1992) is also very useful in providing the political and social context for Merton's life and thought.

Michael Mott's *The Seven Mountains of Thomas Merton* (Boston: Houghton Mifflin, 1984) is the one indispensable book in Merton studies. You need it in hand as you read Merton's own work. The one indispensable guide to Merton himself is his closest friend, Robert Lax. His *journal* C, published in English and German by Pendo in Zurich, speaks directly about Merton shortly after his death in 1968. "i remember the people i loved (who have died) or who've just disappeared—remember their traits as though it were a sacred duty." Lax remembered Merton's traits "as though it were a sacred duty."

Lax talks about Merton's "certainty of tread," his bang-bang-bang walk, and his commitment to write in simple language. Lax's "Harpo's Progress" in Volume I of *The Merton Annual* and his "Remembering Merton & New York" in Volume V of *The Merton Annual* are as close to the flesh and blood of Merton as any writer will ever get. In Lax's "A Poet's Journal," which Mott quotes in his biography, Lax elaborates on the nature of Merton's walk: "he did walk with joy. he walked explosively: bang bang bang, as though fireworks, small & they too, joyful, went off every time his heel hit the ground ... he walked with joy, bounced with joy: knew where he was going." Lax brings Merton to life in loving detail.

On *The Asian Journal*, which I mention in passing here and develop a whole chapter around later (Merton as Journal Keeper), Lax makes this comment, as quoted by James Harford: "best book of Merton's I've read: he's most himself, most keen & observant, witty, lost, (found) erudite, enlightened, clean, natural, free, mature & whatever qualities else are good in man & in Merton."

Lax's "21 pages" in *33 Poems*, edited by Thomas Kellein (New York: New Directions, 1988) is one of the holiest and most deeply spiritual works of the twentieth century. It belongs on the same shelf as Merton's "Hagia Sophia."

George Woodcock uses the choir/desert distinction in his *Thomas Merton: Monk and Poet* (Vancouver: Douglas & McIntyre,

1978) to depict Merton's movement from devotional poetry to a deeper spiritual poetry. He is a man under constant reconstruction. Michael Mott quotes fellow monk Dom John Eudes Bamberger as saying that Merton was "a good self-corrector."

The Kerouac-Merton linkage with other sixties writers occurs in bell hooks, "A Writer in the Village," *Metropolis Found: New York Is Book Country 25th Anniversary Collection* (New York: New York Is Book Country, 2003).

Brother Christopher on *The Seven Storey Mountain* is quoted in *The Book That Changed My Life: 71 Remarkable Writers Celebrate the Books That Matter Most to Them*, edited by Roxanne J. Coady and Joy Johannessen (New York: Gotham Books, 2006).

Edward Rice, pinching in part a phrase from Ernest Hemingway, writes a retrospective on Jubilee called "Starting a Magazine: A Guide for the Courageous—The Short Happy Life of *Jubilee*" in *The Merton Seasonal*, Vol. 24, No. 1, Spring 1999.

In this chapter, and elsewhere, I make reference to the thorough discussion of Merton's art in Roger Lipsey's *Angelic Mistakes: The Art of Thomas Merton* (Boston: New Seeds, 2006).

NO/YES. A very useful, and sometimes neglected, guide to Merton's thinking is contained in *Introductions East & West: The Foreign Prefaces of Thomas Merton*, edited by Robert E. Daggy (Toronto: Mosaic Press, 1981).

Jesus also says yes and no to the world. In Luke 6:20-26 (King James Version) four statements of blessedness are followed by four statements of woe. The poor are blessed, for instance, because theirs is the kingdom of God. The rich, on the other hand, have already received their consolation.

The beginner. Rilke's comment on the beginner is quoted in the introduction to Rainer Maria Rilke, *Selected Poems*, translated with an introduction by J.B. Leishman (London: Penguin, 1964). Significantly, Merton lectured on Rilke to novice monks, read aloud to them significant lines in German from Rilke's poem "The Panther," and connected Rilke's letters to his poems.

Chapter II (Contemplative & Activist)

St. Paul informs Merton's understanding of prayer. In the opening lines of his Epilogue to *Bread in the Wilderness*, Merton points to 1 Corinthians 14-15, "I will pray with the spirit ... I will pray also with the understanding; I will sing with the spirit, I will sing also with the understanding."

The cheese/chant comment comes from Amiya Chakravarty, "Epilogue," as quoted in Donald Grayston and Michael W. Higgins, editors, *Thomas Merton: Pilgrim in Process* (Toronto: Griffin House, 1981).

Brother Patrick Hart conducts a marvellous online interview with Sr. Mary Margaret Funk in http://monasticdialog.com/a. php?id=512: "The Legacy of Thomas Merton," an interview with Br. Patrick Hart, OCSO by Sr. Mary Margaret Funk OSB, Bulletin 74, April 2005. Accessed November 29, 2007.

To enlarge and contextualize Merton's political comment, I make reference to Jim Wallis's *God's Politics: Why the Right Gets It Wrong and the Left Doesn't Get It*; John Dominic Crossan's *God and Empire: Jesus Against Rome, Then and Now*; and Henry Giroux's *Against the New Authoritarianism: Politics after Abu Ghraib*. Giroux paraphrases Lewis Lapham (he could as easily be paraphrasing Merton) to the effect that the right-wing propaganda machine "endlessly grinds out the news that any vestige of the public ... public service, public health, public goods, public life or public schools, is either hopelessly inefficient or simply a relic of Satanic socialism." For the extreme right wing, government seems to have two purposes: make war abroad in the interests of American corporations and build prisons at home for African-Americans, Native Americans, Hispanics, working-class whites and other undesirables. The Bush administration specializes in war, prisons and fear-mongering.

The Dorothy Day quote comes from Robert Coles, *A Robert Coles Omnibus* (Iowa City: University of Iowa Press, 1993). The Mark Van Doren quote is from *The Selected Letters*, edited by George Hendrick (Baton Rouge: Louisiana State University Press, 1987). Van Doren's words are also used in Ross Labrie's *The Art of Thomas Merton* (Fort Worth, TX: The Texas Christian University Press, 1979).

"He gave us the quietness of our minds ... To have dug those utterly simple sentences out of the/soul's grave" are lines from Van Doren's poem to Merton called "Prophet" in *The Selected Letters*.

Rettig's prayer. This prayer is published with the permission of the author, Ted Rettig. It can be found in his bookwork called "sounding things out," edition of 100 copies, copyright 2003, Toronto, Canada.

James W. Douglass, in his Foreword to Merton's *Cold War Letters*, edited by Christine M. Bochen and William H. Shannon (Maryknoll, NY: Orbis Books, 2006), remarks that for Merton "prayer takes many forms. He knew his Cold War Letters were a form of praying in darkness, a search for light with the companions he addressed, in a night of the spirit when everything seemed lost."

One of Merton's most beautiful prayers occurs in *Turning Toward the World, Volume Four, 1960–1963* of his personal journals, edited by Victor A. Kramer:

Lord have mercy.

Have mercy on my darkness, my weakness, my confusion. Have mercy on my infidelity, my cowardice, my turning about in circles, my wandering, my evasions.

I do not ask anything but such mercy, always, in everything, mercy.

My life here—a little solidity and very much ashes.

Almost everything is ashes. What I have prized most is ashes. What I have attended to least, is perhaps, a little solid.

Lord have mercy. Guide me, make me want again to be holy, to be a man of God, even though in desperateness and confusion.

I do not necessarily ask for clarity, a plain way, but only to go according to your love, to follow your mercy, to trust in your mercy.

In *Spirit Book Word: An Inquiry into Literature and Spirituality* (Ottawa: Novalis, 2001), my chapter on Merton centres on his life word, *mercy*.

Chapter III (Poet, Reader, Translator)

I adapt this chapter from my Vancouver talk (2006) at the Vancouver Public Library under the gracious and kind hosting of Rev. Judith Hardcastle. A version of the talk—"Rhinos, Lizards & The Click of Being: Thomas Merton as a Reader of Poetry"—was published in *The Nashwaak Review*, Volume 18/19:1 (Spring/ Summer 2007).

The words of Marcel Proust on reading have application to Merton's philosophy of reading: "Reading is on the threshold of the spiritual life; it can introduce us to it: it does not constitute it." The words are quoted by Mark Edmundson in *Why Read?* (New York: Bloomsbury, 2004). In a letter to M.R. Chandler (July 19, 1963) in *Witness to Freedom: Letters in Times of Crisis*, Merton says, "Traditionally, for a monk, reading is inseparable from *meditation*." In the same volume of letters, Merton writes to L. Dickinson (September 12, 1965) to say that the purpose of education is to enable the student to "establish his true identity." He exhorts the student "to read more widely, more critically, more eagerly, and ... to find books that will revolutionize his life ...."

Merton's own poetry has a place in *Twentieth-Century American Poetry*, edited by Dana Gioia et al. (New York, McGraw-Hill, 2004). The editors include "For My Brother: Reported Missing in Action, 1943" and "The Reader."

Merton's note on translation is in *Learning to Love*, VI.

Merton makes an early remark on Cortés in a letter to José Coronel Urtecho on April 17, 1964: "He is a wonderful and symbolic man, perhaps one of the most significant people of our age ...." In the same letter he acknowledges feeling "very much a part of the Nicaraguan movement in poetry ...." (*Dancing in the Water*, V). Poetically speaking, Nicaragua is the Ireland of Central America, a small country bursting with poets of the highest order. One thinks first of Rubén Darío, the father of modern Nicaraguan poetry, but tumbling into mind quickly thereafter are Cortés, Cuadra and Cardenal.

In a significant and comprehensive anthology entitled *Twentieth-Century Latin American Poetry*, edited by Stephen Tapscott (Austin: University of Texas, 1996), Merton's translations of Vallejo's "Anger," Cuadra's "The Birth of the Sun," Parra's "Mummies," and Cardenal's "Like Empty Beer Cans" are the poems' voices in English.

My Cervantes reference occurs in Jenne Erdal, "Let There Be Light," *The Guardian*, Saturday April 28, 2007: http://books.guardian.co.uk. Accessed November 30, 2007.

Throughout this chapter, I'm indebted to my friend Dale Behnke for walking me through the Spanish.

Stefan Baciu's tribute to Merton is in "The Literary Catalyst," *Continuum*: In Memoriam of Thomas Merton, Volume Seven, Number Two, Summer 1969.

Merton's clearest declaration of reciprocal affection for Latin America occurs in *A Search for Solitude*, III: "My destiny is indeed to be an American—not just an American of the U.S. We are only on the fringe of the True America. I can never be satisfied with this only partial reality that is almost nothing at all ... Never so keenly felt the impermanence of what is now regarded as American because it is *North* American—or the elements of stability and permanence which are in *South* America. Deeper roots, Indian roots. The Spanish, Portuguese Negro roots also. The shallow English roots are not deep enough. The tree will fall ... My vocation is American—*to see and to understand and to have in myself the life and the roots and the belief and the destiny and the Orientation of the whole hemisphere ....*"

In my view, Merton's two fullest and most penetrating literary essays are his "Louis Zukofsky—The Paradise Ear," *The Literary Essays of Thomas Merton* (New York: New Directions, 1981) and his "The True Legendary Sound: The Poetry and Criticism of Edwin Muir," in the same volume.

Larzer Ziff's comment on Emerson is in his Introduction to *Ralph Waldo Emerson: Nature and Selected Essays* (New York: Penguin, 1982).

Chapter IV (Tone Meister)

My thoughts on tone began to take shape in "Thomas Merton & Wendell Berry: A Brief Study in Tone," *The Merton Seasonal* 17.2 (Spring 1992).

Merton speaks of his audience in early journal entries (*Entering the Silence*) as "people in the world, men riding on the Long Island railroad, monks in Irish monasteries, nuns in English convents, my relatives, Jews, reds, priests ... and the people Father Gabriel is afraid to offend." His comment on audience comes forward into his *Sign of Jonas* without the Father Gabriel reference. Did he make slight alterations for *The Sign of Jonas* or did the Church or Order censors make the adjustments?

Both Emerson and Whitman have remarkably personal and direct ways of speaking to their audiences. Their "I" is their listeners' and readers' "I."

Brother Patrick Hart's *First and Last Memories,* with illustrations by Jim Cantrell (Bardstown, KY: Necessity Press, 1986), is a brief and shining jewel.

Everything in Wendell Berry is worth reading. His "Healing" in *What Are People For? Essays* (Berkeley: North Point Press, 1990) is particularly outstanding. His essay on computers in the same volume is, in my view, one-sided.

Chapter V (Letter Writer)

My first thoughts on Merton as a letter writer appeared in a review of *The Courage for Truth: The Letters of Thomas Merton to Writers,* selected and edited by Christine H. Bochen, *Grail* 10.1/2 (1994).

St. Paul is for me the supreme letter writer in world literature. No one else has the same intensity of fire, the same desperate urgency, the same unquenchable thirst. Maybe thorns and shackles and long imprisonment sometimes open unexpected gifts for eloquence.

Psychiatrist Gregory Zilboorg, as quoted in Michael Mott in *The Seven Mountains of Thomas Merton,* offers a very harsh reading of Merton's psychological makeup.

Of Merton's collections of writers, I find *The Hidden Ground of Love* particularly valuable for his intellectual life; *The Road to Joy* valuable for his engagement with young people; *The Courage for Truth* for his writerly contacts; and his co-collection with Lax, *A Catch of Anti-Letters,* for tease and frivolity.

After Merton's death, Czeslaw Milosz remembered him fondly. Daniel Halpern, in *Our Private Lives: Journals, Notebooks, and*

Diaries (New York: Vintage Books, 1990), draws our attention to Milosz thinking in jest that he should write a novel set in Rome. Or, "a monastery like Our Lady of Gethsemani, Kentucky, where people of various professions and views used to come to visit Thomas Merton. Merton himself, with all his contradictory desires, would appear in the novel, not only discussing Duns Scotus with Maritain (who visited him, too) but also thrashing around politically." Milosz also included a Merton poem—"An Elegy for Ernest Hemingway"— in his exquisite poetry anthology, *A Book of Luminous Things: An International Anthology of Poetry* (New York: Harcourt Brace & Company, 1996).

Denise Levertov's poem on Proverb is from *Breathing the Water* (New York: New Directions, 1987). She wrote one other Merton-inspired poem, entitled "On a Theme by Thomas Merton," in her 1993 collection *Evening Train*. I've written about Merton's influence on her work, and on the literary critic Frank Lentricchia, in "Piggybacking on Merton," *Merton Seasonal* 23.2 (Summer 1998).

Chapter VI (Intellectual)

I adapted this chapter from my Vancouver talk in 2003 at Canadian Memorial United Church. Once again, my kind and gracious host was Rev. Judith Hardcastle. The talk was subsequently published as "Thomas Merton as Public Intellectual," *The Merton Seasonal* 29.2 (Summer 2004). A much revised Eichmann article was published in *The Merton Journal: A Journal of the Thomas Merton Society of Great Britain and Ireland*, Guest editor Ross Labrie, Advent 2007: Vol. 14, No. 2.

My daughter, Rachel, and I recently visited Columbia University (May 2007). Much of the university's architecture is unchanged since Merton's day. The Core Curriculum in the arts remains, as does the emphasis on reading the classics. The university continues to offer Humanities C1001-C1002: Masterpieces of Western literature and philosophy, and Contemporary Civilization C1101-C1102: Introduction to contemporary civilization in the west. The Greeks still have a presence on campus in stone and in books. Rachel and I also visited Corpus Christi Church, where Merton was baptized into the Catholic faith. During our visit to New York, I was reading Neal Oxenhandler's *Looking for Heroes in Postwar France* (Hanover: University Press of New England, 1966), where Oxenhandler remarks that Simone Weil "attended Mass daily at the small brick church of Corpus Christi where Thomas Merton was baptized ...." Sometimes by serendipity one reads the right book at the right time.

George Steiner's delightful comment about intellectuals being readers with pencils is found in *No Passion Spent: Essays 1978–1995* (New Haven: Yale University Press, 1996).

For Merton's intellectual background and context, Robert Inchausti's *Thomas Merton's American Prophecy* (Albany, NY: State University of New York Press, 1998) is a worthwhile read.

I take my paraphrase of Saint Teresa from Tess Gallagher's Introduction to Raymond Carver's *A New Path to the Waterfall* (New York: The Atlantic Monthly Press, 1989).

Morris Berman's idea of "the monastic option" occurs in *The Twilight of American Culture* (New York: Norton, 2000); he shows no sign of being familiar with Merton's hermitage, or Ernesto Cardenal's Christian commune on an archipelago of 38 islands in Lake Nicaragua, or Brother Enzo Bianchi's mixed ecumenical monastic community in Bose, Italy.

The Palestinian-American Edward Said says more about the moral role of intellectuals in public life in his *Representations of the Intellectual*, the 1993 Reith Lectures (London: Vintage, 1994), than a hundred pontificators and prevaricators. His *The World, the Text and the Critic* (Cambridge: Harvard University Press, 1983) is equally outstanding. His essay in *The World* on Jonathan Swift is the single best thing that I have ever read on the Irish satirist.

A very useful book to elucidate the octopus-reach of technology is Neil Postman's *Technopoly: The Surrender of Culture to Technology* (New York: Vintage Books, 1993).

The Eichmann biography I refer to throughout this chapter is David Cesarani, *Eichmann: His Life and Crimes* (London: William Heinemann, 2004).

As a guide through the Eichmann thicket, there is no one better than Hannah Arendt in *Eichmann in Jerusalem: A Report on the Banality of Evil* (New York: Viking Press, 1964). *The Portable Hannah Arendt*, edited with an introduction by Peter Baehr (New York: Viking Press, 2000) is also necessary reading.

I draw extensively from Merton's *Passion for Peace: The Social Essays*, edited and introduced by William H. Shannon (New York: The Crossroad Publishing Company, 1995), throughout my discussion of Eichmann.

I'm grateful to Michael W. Higgins in *Heretic Blood: The Spiritual Geography of Thomas Merton* (Toronto: Stoddart, 1998) for his connecting Swiftian technique to Merton's artistic treatment of Eichmann.

Gosnia Poks in Poland writes to inform me that "Chant to Be Used in Processions around a Site with Furnaces" builds on Hess rather than Eichmann. She correctly points out that in his letter to Lawrence Ferlinghetti (August 2, 1961) Merton says that he didn't so much have Eichmann in mind as "the commandant of Auschwitz, [Rudolf] Hess." The commandant of Auschwitz, however, was Rudolf Hoess. Whether Merton's inspiration derives from Eichmann or Hess or Hoess or all three together, Merton's *Chant* is a powerful distillation of Nazi thought and speech.

Sometimes poetry carries insight difficult to reach by other means. The Eichmann poems in Leonard Cohen's *Selected Poems 1956–1968* (Toronto: McClelland and Stewart, 1969) and Denise Levertov's *Selected Poems* (New York: New Directions, 2002) are important additions to our understanding of a Nazi officer. Merton's own poetic re-creations of Eichmann are, in my estimation, unparalleled in Eichmann studies.

Chapter VII (Lover)

Both Jim Forest and Michael Higgins write with great skill and insight into Merton's lunge for love. Mott, as always, is indispensable, as is Christine M. Bochen's introduction to *Learning to Love*, VI.

Merton's *Love and Living*, edited by Naomi Burton Stone and Brother Patrick Hart, is useful to hold in one hand while you read his love journal in the other. His essays "Learning to Live" and "Love and Need: Is Love a Package or a Message?" from *Love and Living* clearly show the power and influence of M on his thinking. In his riff on falling in love, Merton says that you "fall" "when you are carried off by a power beyond your control. Once you start, you can't stop. You're gone." He also emphasizes that love "*is a certain special way of being alive*"; it is "an intensification of life, a completeness, a fullness, a wholeness of life." I do not believe that Merton could have arrived at the strength and clarity of these words without his love for M.

The comment by Joan Baez is in John Howard Griffin's *Follow the Ecstasy: Thomas Merton, The Hermitage Years, 1965–1968* (JHG Editions/Latitudes Press, 1983).

I've paraphrased Merton's dreams from *Learning to Love*, VI. There are many other dreams related to M in the journal that I haven't made use of. Most of the dreams have to do with the thwarting of desire.

The rose dream doesn't involve M directly. Merton dreams of another girl, but what remains significant is that his Mother—he capitalizes mother—blocks him from fulfilling his desire.

In a letter to Sister Anita (December 10, 1967), Merton speaks retrospectively of his hospitalization and his affair of the heart: "... I was in a state of helplessness for a couple of days and it almost threw me. When someone came along with an enormous amount of tender and devoted care, it made an impression. We were both set up for it, without knowing it, and before we could really give it a thought, we were in love." He dishonours M with these words: "Where I made the mistake was of course in continuing to see her after I got out of the hospital. Time has taken care of it. She moved from Louisville, and I have more or less stopped communicating with her." He then disingenuously adds: "I hope she isn't mad at me for that ...." M, it seems to me, was not a mistake but a blessing.

All Merton readers are thankful to editor Lynn R. Szabo and New Directions for making most of the *Eighteen Poems*, Merton's love poems, available at a reasonable price. No serious reader of Merton would want to be without *In the Dark Before the Dawn: New Selected Poems of Thomas Merton* (New York: New Directions, 2005).

Margaret Visser reminds us in her Massey Lecture entitled *Beyond Fate* (Toronto: Anansi, 2002) that Canadian theologian Bernard Lonergan formulated five Transcendental Precepts: attentiveness, intelligence, reasonableness, responsibility and love. Merton experienced, and acted on, all five precepts but not always at the same time.

Chapter VIII (Synthesizer)

My thoughts on Merton and the self were first published as "Thomas Merton's Late Metaphors of the Self," in *The Merton Annual* 7 (1994).

Merton's "I write, therefore, I am" may have more than metaphoric significance. Ivan Illich, in his illuminating study co-authored with Barry Saunders, *ABC: The Alphabetization of the Popular Mind*

(New York: Vintage Books, 1989), informs readers that "the idea of a self ... cannot exist without the text. Where there is no alphabet, there can neither be a memory ... nor the 'I' as its appointed watchman."

Autobiography as an orphan art form. English art critic, novelist and memoirist John Berger explores this idea in *Keeping a Rendezvous* (New York: Pantheon Books, 1991).

Canadian philosopher Charles Taylor thoroughly investigates selfhood in *Sources of the Self: The Making of the Modern Identity* (Cambridge: Harvard University Press, 1989).

Guy Davenport makes his arresting comment on the protean Merton in Ralph Eugene Meatyard's *Father Louie: Photographs of Thomas Merton*, edited by Barry Magrid (New York: Timken, 1991).

"The self as a reference point and a belonging field" is a remark attributed to Gerard Manley Hopkins in *A Hopkins Reader*, edited by John Pick (Garden City, NY: Image Books, 1966).

David D. Cooper speaks authoritatively on Merton's integration and sometimes lack thereof in *Thomas Merton's Art of Denial: The Evolution of a Radical Humanist* (Athens and London: The University of Georgia Press, 1989).

Where Merton himself seems to develop his clearest ideas of the self is in *Ishi Means Man: Essays on Native Americans* (Greensboro, NC: Unicorn, 1976).

A very readable and accessible biography of The Buddha that discusses his ideas of selfhood is Michael Carrithers's *The Buddha* (Oxford: Oxford University Press, 1983).

Merton develops his ideas of final integration in "Final Integration: Toward A Monastic Therapy," *Contemplation in a World of Action* (New York: Doubleday, 1973).

Ron Dart makes interesting connections between Merton and Kerouac and the other Beats in *Thomas Merton and the Beats of the North Cascades* (North Vancouver, BC: Prospect Press, 2005).

Professor Jacques Goulet develops his point on the early Merton's aggression and exclusivity with great clarity in his paper "Thomas Merton's Journey Toward World Religious Ecumenism" in *The Merton Annual* 4 (New York: AMS Press, 1992).

Merton speaks of the need for idols to go into the fire in his address to novice monks in "The True and False Self," AA2267, (Kansas City: Credence Cassettes, 1990).

Chapter IX (Journal Keeper)

I adapt this chapter from my article "The Last Journals of Thomas Merton & Anaïs Nin," *The Merton Annual* 5 (1992).

I make use of Deidre Bair's talk "The French Sensualists— Colette and Nin," a lecture delivered at the International Festival of Authors (Harbourfront, Toronto, October 19, 1990), throughout my discussion of Nin.

My Nin quotes are primarily from her last journal, *The Diary of Anaïs Nin 1966–1974*, Vol. VII, edited by Gunther Stuhlmann (San Diego: Harcourt Brace Jovanovich, 1980). Most Merton quotes are from his last journal, *The Asian Journal of Thomas Merton*, edited from his original notebooks by Naomi Burton, Brother Patrick Hart & James Laughlin (New York: New Directions, 1975).

For Merton, the perfect form would seem to be a kind of scrapbook, even a kind of Facebook, in which prayers, photographs, drawings, memories, ideas, polemics and poems all co-exist com- fortably in a common space. One thinks of Doris Lessing's *The Golden Notebook*, where the character Anna keeps four differently coloured notebooks: a black one for her African experiences; a red one for politics; a yellow one for a novel; a blue one for a personal diary. Finally, she begins a golden notebook in which she tries to bind the threads and concerns of all four books.

Aside from *The Asian Journal*, the closest thing to a scrapbook or Facebook in Merton is *Monks Pond: Thomas Merton's Little Magazine*, edited with an introduction by Robert E. Daggy (Lexington, KY: The University of Kentucky Press, 1989). As editor, Merton includes photography (often his own but sometimes Ralph Eugene Meatyard's), poetry, art manifestoes, proverbs, myths, philosophic and psychological essays, literary criticism, spiritual explorations, and translations in his journal of four seasons. Even though Merton is more selector than writer for the journal, his *Monks Pond* is nevertheless a mirror of his mind. In 1968, he writes to Wendell Berry who provides, among other things, spectacular haiku for the journal: "I don't think a monastic press should be confined to cheese and liturgy." What he desired for the journal—"One brief magazine flash in the air and out ...."—he accomplished. Only 150 to 200 copies of each issue were printed, according to Daggy's introduction.

Chapter X (Hello, Goodbye, Hello Again)

An earlier version of my ambivalence appeared in "Farewell to a Monk," *The Antigonish Review* 108 (Winter 1997).

The Merton-Kerouac connection consists of more than style. A boy's joy runs through their probes and pronouncements. Kerouac is more prone to depression following manic highs, but both race headlong into ecstasy. Merton is more disciplined and less self-destructive, but both enjoy people on the margins, people without official status in the world. Both are tremendously visual as well as verbal. Merton draws and photographs, and Kerouac paints and draws. They're both rebellious at times. Obeying authority doesn't come easily to either. Merton's English headmaster once described him in these words: "He was something of a legendary figure among the old boys of his generation and he was clearly something of a rebel." William H. Shannon quotes these words in his *Thomas Merton: An Introduction* (Cincinnati, OH: St. Anthony Messenger Press, 1997, 2005). Michael W. Higgins calls his study of Merton *Heretic Blood.*

Another major difference between Merton and Kerouac is that Merton spent his day, as a practising Trappist, in silence or in writing about it. Some of the happiest-looking photographs are of Kerouac holding court in a bar. It's not difficult to imagine Merton in similar surroundings, but silence, nevertheless, was a more central part of his life. His life was in accord with British art critic Sister Wendy Beckett's words in *Meditations on Silence* (Mississauga, ON: Fern Publishing, 1995): "What silence principally armors us against is Babel: the endless foolish chatter, words used to confound thought, words misused to ward off friendship or attachments, words as occupation."

Merton felt that an act of mercy enabled him, despite natural proclivities towards loquaciousness and gregariousness, to maintain a life of silence and solitude. The silence was, of course, intercut with talk at times, and the solitude by company. Curiously, Kerouac also aspired to a kind of monkhood. Ed Adler quotes a July 14, 1955, letter to Allen Ginsberg in *Departed Angels: The Last Paintings* (New York: Thunder's Mouth Press, 2004): "Turns out that all my final favorite writers (Dickinson, Blake, Thoreau)"—This could be Merton speaking—"ended up their lives in little hermitages … Emily in her cottage, Blake in his, with wife; and Thoreau his hut … This I think will be my truly final move … tho I don't know where yet. It depends on how much money I can get. If I had all the money in the world, I would still prefer a humble hut. I guess in Mexico. Al Sublette once said what I wanted was a thatched hut in Lowell." Kerouac's hut ended up being his mother's house.

In the same way that one can see Kerouac's spontaneity in Merton's journals, one can also see Ad Reinhardt's influence on Merton's artwork. The first entry of volume one of *Monks Pond* is the reprinting of Reinhardt's "ART – AS – ART." One sees connections between Reinhardt's manifesto and Merton's musings in "Signatures: Notes on the Author's Drawings" and in his "Answers to Art and Freedom." Reinhardt says in one of his statements: "The one work ... Nothing 'useable', 'manipulatable', 'saleable', 'dealable', 'collectable', 'graspable'. No art as a commodity or a jobbery. Art is not the spiritual side of business." The words could be Merton's. Reinhardt's words—"... one symmetry, one texture, one formal device, one free-hand-brushing, one rhythm, one working everything into one dissolution and one indivisibility ..."—seem to speak to the origin and purpose of Merton's abstract ink drawings and prints.

For my final chapter, I rely on Ron Seitz's *A Memory Vision*, Edward Said's *On Late Style: Music and Literature Against the Grain* (New York: Pantheon Books, 2006), and Jack Kerouac's novel *Desolation Angels*.

I draw on Roger Lipsey's *Angelic Mistakes* and Robert Lax's vision of Merton's life and work in *A Catch of Anti-Letters*. Lax repeats his emphasis on Merton's integrated wholeness in "Harpo's Progress." I also quote John Berger's *And our faces, my heart, as brief as photos* (New York: Pantheon Books, 1984).

The Merton quotes come from his *Catch of Anti-Letters* with Lax; his "Signatures" in *Raids on the Unspeakable*; his *Foreign Prefaces*; his *Sign of Jonas*; his "First and Last Thoughts" in *A Thomas Merton Reader*, revised edition, edited by Thomas P. McDonnell (New York: Doubleday, 1974, 1989); his *New Seeds of Contemplation*; and his *Turning toward the World*, IV.

Behind my reading is the inspirational *A Year with Thomas Merton: Daily Meditations from His Journals*, selected and edited by Jonathan Montaldo (San Francisco: HarperSanFrancisco, 2004). I also take to heart Merton's letter to L. Dickson (September 12, 1965) containing these words: "You cannot go through life as a mask or as a well-functioning biological machine. Man is a being whose reality cannot be left entirely to forces outside himself, nature, society, events. We become real in proportion as we accept the real possibilities that are presented to us, and *choose from them freely and realistically* for ourselves." Merton is seldom anything less than real.

I also make reference to my own documentary poetic reprojection of Merton, called *The Thomas Merton Poems* (Goderich, ON: Moonstone Press, 1988). My prose poem "Thomas Merton in Las Vegas" was published in *The Merton Seasonal* 16: 3 (Summer 1991).

Merton's book on the Psalms, *Bread in the Wilderness*, is, in my view, much superior in style and substance to his *Opening the Bible*. He dives more deeply into the mysteries. He plants his body more firmly on the page.

In Cold War Letter 103 to Catholic theologian Leslie Dewart (September 1962), Merton waxes clairvoyantly on "the American mentality," which he regards as "involved in deep illusions, most of all about itself." He excoriates the principal American illusion of "the earthly paradise," where "everyone recovers original goodness." He exposes the "illusion of innocence," a theme other great American writers from Hawthorne to Melville to Henry James to Philip Roth have similarly struck. All look clear-headedly at "the human stain," and the American stain in particular. Merton's analysis thrums with accuracy and energy: "[B]ecause we are prosperous, because we are successful, because we have all this amazing 'know-how' (without real intelligence or moral wisdom, without even a really deep scientific spirit) we are entitled to defend ourselves by any means whatever, without any limitation, and all the more so because what we are defending is our illusion of innocence." Has anyone else brought the Bush Doctrine on pre-emptive strikes to clarity in such few words? In American foreign policy, evil is externalized—think of the Evil Empire or the Axis of Evil—as in Hawthorne's *The Scarlet Letter* and Melville's *Moby Dick*, and violence is perpetrated on the other in order to protect the illusion of one's innocence.

Merton's death is honoured in *A Merton Concelebration*, tributes from friends of the poet-monk, edited by Deba Prasad Patnaik (Notre Dame, IN: Ave Maria Press, 1981). Among the celebrants is Robert Lax, who in "A Poem for Thomas Merton" offers these words:

SIN
GU
LAR

STAR

SIN
GU
LAR

CLOUD

SIN
GU
LAR

HILL ...

ONE
HILL

ONE
CLOUD

ONE
STAR

Is Lax playfully invoking Reinhardt's manifesto's emphasis on one—"one art," "one history," "one evolution," etc.?

Brother Patrick Hart, Merton's personal secretary in the final years of his life, comments in the Preface to Deba Patnaik's compilation of tributes that the book reminds him of the "joy and enthusiasm" with which Merton undertook his own editing of *Monks Pond*, when he invited friends and poets from far and near to make evanescent contributions to a deliberately conceived ephemeral journal.

Merton's Works Cited

Asian Journal, The. New York: New Directions, 1973.

At Home in the World: The Letters of Thomas Merton & Rosemary Radford Ruether, ed. Mary Tardiff, OP. Maryknoll, NY: Orbis, 1995.

Bread in the Wilderness. New York: New Directions, 1953.

Catch of Anti-Letters, A, with Robert Lax. Kansas City, KS: Sheed Andrews & McMeel, 1978.

Cold War Letters, eds. Christine M. Bochen and William H. Shannon. Maryknoll, NY: Orbis, 2006.

Collected Poems of Thomas Merton, The. New York: New Directions, 1973.

Conjectures of a Guilty Bystander. Garden City, NY: Doubleday, 1966.

Contemplation in a World of Action. Garden City, NY: Doubleday, 1971.

Courage for Truth, The: The Letters of Thomas Merton to Writers, ed. Christine M. Bochen. New York: Farrar, Straus and Giroux, 1993.

Dancing in the Water of Life: Seeking Peace in the Hermitage, Journals of Thomas Merton, vol. 5, 1963–1965, ed. Robert E. Daggy. San Francisco: HarperSanFrancisco, 1997.

Day of a Stranger. Introduction by Robert E. Daggy. Salt Lake City: Gibbs M. Smith, 1981.

Disputed Questions. New York: Farrar, Straus & Cudahy, 1960.

Emblems of a Season of Fury. New York: New Directions, 1963.

Entering the Silence: Becoming a Monk and Writer: Journals of Thomas Merton, vol. 2, 1941–1952, ed. Jonathan Montaldo. San Francisco: HarperSanFrancisco, 1996.

Geography of Holiness: The Photography of Thomas Merton, ed. Deba Prasad Patnaik. New York: Pilgrim Press, 1980.

Hidden Ground of Love, The. The Letters of Thomas Merton on Religious Experience and Social Concerns, selected and edited by William H. Shannon. New York: Harcourt, 1993.

In the Dark Before Dawn: New Selected Poems of Thomas Merton, ed. Lynn R. Szabo. New York: New Directions, 2005.

Intimate Merton, The. His Life from His Journals, ed. Patrick Hart, O.C.S.O. and Jonathan Montaldo. San Francisco: HarperSanFrancisco, 1999.

Ishi Means Man: Essays on Native Americans. Greensboro, NC: Unicorn Press, 1976.

Learning to Love: Exploring Solitude and Freedom: Journals of Thomas Merton, vol. 6, 1966–1967, ed. Christine M. Bochen. San Francisco: HarperSanFrancisco, 1997.

Literary Essays of Thomas Merton, The, ed. Brother Patrick Hart, O.C.S.O. New York: New Directions, 1981.

Love and Living, eds. Naomi Burton Stone and Brother Patrick Hart. New York: Farrar, Straus and Giroux, 1979.

Monks Pond: Thomas Merton's Little Magazine, ed. Robert E. Daggy. Lexington, KY: University Press of Kentucky, 1989.

My Argument with the Gestapo: A Macaronic Journal [original title, *Journal of My Escape from the Nazis*]. Garden City, NY: Doubleday, 1969.

Mystics and Zen Masters. New York: Farrar, Straus and Giroux, 1967.

New Seeds of Contemplation. Norfolk, CT: New Directions, 1962.

Opening the Bible. Collegeville, MN: Liturgical Press, 1970.

Other Side of the Mountain: The End of the Journey: Journals of Thomas Merton, vol. 7, 1967–1968, ed. Patrick Hart, O.C.S.O. San Francisco: HarperSanFrancisco, 1998.

Passion for Peace: The Social Essays of Thomas Merton, ed. William H. Shannon. New York: Crossroad, 1995.

Raids on the Unspeakable. New York: New Directions, 1966.

Road to Joy, The: Letters to New and Old Friends, ed. Robert E. Daggy. New York: Farrar, Straus and Giroux, 1989.

Run to the Mountain: The Story of a Vocation: Journals of Thomas Merton, vol. 1, 1939–1960, ed. Brother Patrick Hart, O.C.S.O. San Francisco: HarperSanFrancisco, 1995.

School of Charity, The: Letters on Religious Renewal and Spiritual Direction, ed. Brother Patrick Hart, O.C.S.O. New York: Farrar, Straus and Giroux, 1990.

Search for Solitude, A: Pursuing the Monk's True Life: Journals of Thomas Merton, vol. 3, 1952–1960, ed. Lawrence S. Cunningham. San Francisco: HarperSanFrancisco, 1996.

Secular Journal of Thomas Merton, The. New York: Farrar, Straus & Cudahy, 1959.

Seven Storey Mountain, The. New York: Harcourt Brace, 1948.

Sign of Jonas, The. New York: Harcourt Brace, 1953.

Thomas Merton: Essential Writings, selected with an introduction by Christine M. Bochen. Orbis: Maryknoll, NY: 2000.

Thomas Merton Reader, A, ed.Thomas P. McDonnell. New York: Doubleday, 1974.

Thomas Merton: Spiritual Master: The Essential Writings, ed. Lawrence S. Cunningham. Mahwah, NJ: Paulist Press, 1992.

Turning Toward the World: The Pivotal Years: Journals of Thomas Merton, vol. 4, 1960–1963, ed. Victor A. Kramer. San Francisco: HarperSanFrancisco, 1996.

Vow of Conversation, A: Journal, 1964–65, ed. Naomi Burton Stone. New York: Farrar, Straus and Giroux, 1988.

Way of Chuang Tzu, The. New York: New Directions, 1965.

When the Trees Say Nothing: Writings on Nature, ed. Kathleen Deignan. Notre Dame, IN: Sorin Books, 2003.

Witness to Freedom: Letters of Thomas Merton in Times of Crisis, ed. William H. Shannon. New York: Farrar, Straus and Giroux, 1994.

Zen and the Birds of Appetite. New York: New Directions, 1968.

Important Dates
on the Merton Calendar

1915 – born January 31st in Prades, France, of artistic parents.

1916 – moves to the United States to be with his mother's family.

1921 – his mother dies of cancer.

1925 – returns to France for his early schooling.
 –26

1928 – attends school in England.

1931 – his father dies of a brain tumour.

1933 – studies at Cambridge (modern languages, French and Italian).

1934 – returns to the United States.

1935 – enters Columbia University where he completes a master's in English on William Blake; friendship with Professor Mark Van Doren.

1937 – at Columbia, editor of 1937 *Yearbook*, art editor of Columbia University *Jester*; readings in Eastern religions and philosophies, interest in the spiritual life; friendships with Robert Lax, Ed Rice, Sy Freedgood, Robert Giroux, etc.

Thomas Merton

1938 – meeting with Brahmachari; received into the Catholic Church at Corpus Christi church; meeting with Dan Walsh, professor of philosophy at Columbia; book reviews for *New York Times*, *New York Herald Tribune* until 1940.

1940– teaches English at St. Bonaventure University; meets
–41 Catherine de Hueck (Doherty) and visits Friendship House in Harlem, NY; trip to Cuba.

1941 – enters the Abbey of Our Lady of Gethsemani on December 10th.

1943 – death of his brother, John Paul.

1944 – simple vows; his first book of poetry, *Thirty Poems*.

1947 – solemn vows.

1948 – *The Seven Storey Mountain*.

1949 – ordained a priest.

1951 – Master of Scholastics (teaching students for the priesthood)
–55

1953 – *The Sign of Jonas*.

1954 – meets Victor Hammer.

1955 – Master of Novices (more teaching).
–65

1957 – friendship with Ernesto Cardenal, a novice at Gethsemani.

1961 – meets John Howard Griffin; photography started with Griffin's camera.

1962 – *New Seeds of Contemplation*; meeting with Dan Berrigan; *Original Child Bomb* (prose poem).

1963 – *Emblems of a Season of Fury*.

1964 – meets D.T. Suzuki in New York City.

1965 – *The Way of Chuang Tzu.*

1965 – lives as a hermit on the grounds of the monastery.
–68

1966 – *Conjectures of a Guilty Bystander; Raids on the Unspeakable;* meetings with Jacques Maritain, Joan Baez and Thich Nhat Hanh.

1968 – edits *Monks Pond;* writes *Zen and the Birds of Appetite.*

1968 – dies in Bangkok, Thailand, on December 10th; burial at the Abbey of Gethsemani December 17th.

I'm indebted to Christine M. Bochen for her Orbis book in the Modern Spiritual Masters Series entitled *Thomas Merton: Essential Writings;* William H. Shannon's critical biography, *Silent Lamp: The Thomas Merton Story;* and *A Merton Concelebration,* edited by Deba Patnaik, for my reconstruction of significant dates in Merton's life.

Acknowledgments

I continue to draw strength and inspiration from my father, Rev. John Porter. He is my ever-present great encourager.

Thank you to my Portavogie mother, Anna (Mahood) Porter, who wisely insisted that I conclude this book with "Hello, Goodbye, Hello Again"; my wife, Cheryl, for constant love and patience; my sister Caroline and brother-in-law Andy for their steadfast loyalty; and my children, Daniel and Rachel, and their partners, Wanh and Steve, for keeping me young.

For their encouragement, I thank my mother-in-law, Lillian Wisdom, and my friends Dale Behnke, Wayne Allan, David Wagg, David Cohen, Marilyn Gear Pilling, Dan Pilling, Sue Carroll, Wes Snihur and Bryan Prince in Hamilton; Judith Hardcastle, Elaine Perry, Susan McCaslin, Ross Labrie, David and Ashley McGhee, and Ron Dart in Vancouver; Bronwyn Drainie, Helen Walsh, B.W. Powe and Ted Rettig in Toronto; Anne and Bob McPherson in St. Catharines; Eileen McGowan in Oshawa; Patrick F. O'Connell in Erie, PA; Paul Pearson in Louisville; Ron Haflidson in Halifax; António Dinis Lopes in Lisbon; and Michael and Krystyna Higgins in Fredericton. If you need a village to raise a child, you need cities to grow a book.

I am especially grateful to Marilyn Gear Pilling for her suggestion that I should begin *Hermit* with how I began to read Merton, and her husband, Dan Pilling, for his concept of the Zorba monk. I thank Dale Behnke for his help in translating Alfonso Cortés's Spanish into English.

I heartily thank Kevin Burns, the editorial director of Novalis, for his faith in the book, and his work on it. His personal and intimate photography—Mertonian in its vision—is also much appreciated. Thanks also to Anne Louise Mahoney, the managing editor of Novalis, for her invaluable work on the manuscript. Both editors possess Daniel's courage and Job's patience, perhaps even Solomon's wisdom.

This book has been printed on 100% post consumer
waste paper, certified Eco-logo and processed chlorine free.

100%